Citizenship
Studies

for OCR GCSE Short Course

Tony Thorpe
David Marsh

INDIVIDUALS ENGAGING IN SOCIETY Citizenship Foundation

With contribution from Tony Breslin,
Ted Huddleston, Dan Mace, Jan Newton,
Don Rowe and Carrie Supple

Hodder & Stoughton
A MEMBER OF THE HODDER HEADLINE GROUP

In this book, we have, to the best of our knowledge, described the law as it stood on 1 July 2002. However, in trying to summarise and simplify the law we have had to leave out some legal details. Therefore, this book cannot be taken as proof of your legal rights. It will be important in some circumstances to seek further advice before taking any action.

The Citizenship Foundation is an independent educational charity that aims to help young people and adults become more effective citizens through a better understanding of law and society.

It produces a range of publications and resources, including the award-winning *Young Citizen's Passport*, a practical pocket guide to the law, which can be used in conjunction with this book. Further information and details of its activities can be found on the Citizenship Foundation's website at www.citfou.org.uk. The Citizenship Foundation, Ferroners House, Shaftesbury Place (off Aldersgate Street) London EC2Y 8AA, tel 020 7367 0500, e-mail info@citfou.org.uk

Editors: Jan Newton and Don Rowe

The authors and editors are very grateful for the support they have received from Hodder & Stoughton and OCR in the preparation of this book and would also particularly like to thank the following for their help and guidance: Margery Allan, Mark Askam, Janet Atfield, Sandra Bell, Rupert Boddington, Michael Callanan, Steve Connolly, Ian Davies, Janet Edwards, Laura Emms, Mike Gibas, Sheila Harding, Keith Hardy, Wally Harbert, the Beth Johnson Foundation, Dala Kundi, Lena Lo, Andrew Lockstone, John Malyon, Mike Moores, Diane Pearson, Cheryl Rehal, Heather Scott, Mike Spencer JP, Lesley Staff, Annie Stevenson, Nigel West and the staff of Doncaster library.

The publisher would like to thank the following for permission to reproduce copyright images in this book:

Associated Press/Reuters: p18 (br); p74 (r) Boris Grdanoski; p77 Santiago Lyon; p20 (tl). Corbis: p74 (l) Hulton Deutsch Collection; p79 Howard Davies; p124 Wolfgang Kaehler. Rex Features: p51 Peter MacDiarmid; p60 (t) Lindsey Parnaby; p97 (r) PGI; p103 Rex. PA News: p65 Lindsey Parnaby; PA Photos: p14 Tony Harris; PA Photos: p18 (bl) EPA; p21; p58 Michael Stephens; p60 (b) John Giles; p73 (r) Phil Noble; p74 EPA; p80 John Giles; p97 (l) Barry Batchelor; p97 EPA; p109 Paul Faith; p101 David Jones; p107 Toby Melville; p111 Michael Stephens; p112 Neil Munns; p118 (l) Matthew Fearn; p119; p120 EPA; Photofusion: p14 Gina Glover. Popperfoto: p100. Topham Picturepoint: p34 Observer. John Grooms: p67. Mary Evans Picture Library: p82. Childline: p86. Kidscape: p86. NSPCC: p86. Bristol City Council; South West News Service: p104. Mo Wilson/Format: p94. Andrew Thorpe: p32. TOGRAFOX: p88 Bob Battersby. Photodisc: pp 4, 5, 6, 7, 10, 13, 15, 22, 23, 25, 28, 29, 37, 38, 39, 40, 41, 42, 43, 45, 54, 55, 61, 62, 63, 67, 68, 69, 71, 73, 75, 78, 81, 83, 85, 86, 90, 91, 92, 93, 94, 95, 96, 99, 111, 117, 120, 121, 123, 124, 125, 126, 127, 131, 132, 133. Digital Image Ingram Publishing: pp 5, 7, 9, 23, 38, 40, 43, 45, 50, 62, 69, 84, 85, 94, 95, 99, 106, 121, 123, 133. Corel: pp 61, 72, 75. Illustrated London News: pp 64, 72, 81,118. Ikon Imaging: pp 12, 17, 65. Eyewire: pp13, 22, 23, 65, 76, 91. ImageBoss: pp 7, 9, 42, 90. Think Stock: p30. Digital Vision: pp 107, 123, 125. Metropolitan Police: p6. Nomad Graphique: pp 7, 37, 39, 40, 54, 84, 92–3, 99, 101, 108, 113. Citizenship Foundation: p9. Letchworth Garden City Heritage Foundation: pp 50, 32, 33. Council of Europe: p19.

Every effort has been made to trace and acknowledge ownership of copyright. The Publishers will be glad to make suitable arrangements with any copyright holders whom it has not been possible to contact.

Orders: please contact Bookpoint Ltd, 130 Milton Park, Abingdon, Oxon OX14 4SB. Telephone: (44) 01235 827720, Fax: (44) 01235 400454. Lines are open from 9.00 - 6.00, Monday to Saturday, with a 24 hour message answering service.
You can also order through our website www.hodderheadline.co.uk

British Library Cataloguing in Publication Data
A catalogue record for this title is available from The British Library

ISBN 0 340 84521X

First published 2002
Impression number   10   9   8   7   6   5   4
Year   2007 2006 2005 2004

Copyright ©2002 The Citizenship Foundation

Design, artwork and typesetting by Nomad Graphique.
Printed in Italy for Hodder & Stoughton Educational, a division of Hodder Headline, 338 Euston Road, London NW1 3BH.

Contents

Citizenship Studies

In these introductory pages we look at the meaning of the words *citizen* and *citizenship*.

Starting out

■ What's it all about?

If you told someone at home that you had maths or French this afternoon, they would probably have a reasonably good idea about what you would be doing.

Maths, French, physics etc. are subjects that have been studied at school for such a long time that everyone has at least some idea of what they cover.

Citizenship Studies, however, is different. It doesn't have the ring of familiarity of most subjects. It has appeared on the curriculum only recently.

A further difficulty lies with the meaning of the words in the subject title. What does *citizenship* mean?

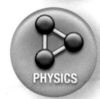

■ Citizens and citizenship

Your answers to these questions probably didn't just describe a citizen as someone living in society, but also contained ideas of them taking part and belonging. This was how Aristotle, a writer and thinker living in Ancient Greece in the fourth century BC, described a citizen. A citizen, he said is *one who has a share in both ruling and being ruled.*

Although life in Ancient Greece was very different from the way in which people live today, Aristotle's definition is still useful in conveying the idea that the meaning of citizenship carries ideas of rights and responsibilities.

In Citizenship Studies you will look at these rights and responsibilities against the background of what is happening in society today. You will be asked to consider many topical issues on which people disagree. You will also look at how the law works, at how important decisions in society are made, and at how ordinary citizens can influence what is going on.

? questions

1. Working in small groups of three or four, write down the word *citizen* and then jot down any words that you associate with it. There are no wrong answers here.

    Share your ideas with another group, or the whole class. Draw up a complete list of suggestions.

2. Now use the words on your list to write down two different statements that explain something about being a citizen.

    Begin each statement in the following way:
    a) A citizen is ....
    b) A good citizen is .....

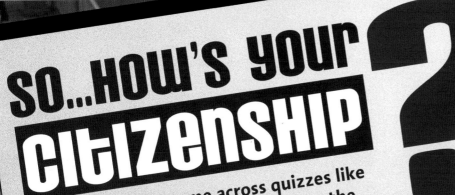

SO...HOW'S YOUR CITIZENSHIP?

You've probably come across quizzes like this before. How would you answer the following questions?

1 From what age will you be old enough to vote in a general election?
a) 16 years
b) 18 years
c) 21 years

2 You buy a new DVD player from a local superstore. You take it home and it doesn't work. What would you do?
a) Take it back to the store.
b) Send it back to the manufacturer.
c) Get a friend to fix it.

3 You have been working for the same company for two years. Your old boss is replaced by a new manager, who sacks you without warning. What do you do?
a) Try to get another job.
b) Confront the boss and ask why you have lost your job.
c) Take the company to an employment tribunal.

4 You discover the new trainers that you so badly want are made by overseas workers on very low wages. What do you do?
a) Refuse to buy them as a protest.
b) Buy them, but moan to the shop assistant.
c) Buy them - saying to yourself that there is not much you can do about it.

5 A friend at school offers to sell you some drugs. You turn them down. What do you do next?
a) Speak about the matter with a teacher with whom you get on well.
b) Tell him not to be so stupid.
c) Nothing.

6 You have been asked by a friend to join her doing some voluntary work at a club for young children. What do you do?
a) Say you think it's a great idea.
b) Say that you don't really want to help.
c) Explain that you are already involved in a number of things and you honestly don't have time.

7 You are on holiday in Spain and you have made friends with a group of German and Spanish teenagers. They ask you how you feel about the Euro. What do you say?
a) You think Manchester United will win again.
b) The sooner we sort our trains out the better.
c) You think the single currency is a good or bad idea (depending on your own point of view).

Citizenship Studies

Answers

skills

knowledge

confidence

■ Your view

There is no mark scheme for this quiz. While there is a correct answer to some questions – such as *b) 18 years* in question 1 – there are others in which two, or even all three, answers could be right. Selecting the most appropriate would often depend on the circumstances at the time.

Although this book will give you information about law, politics and the way in which we behave, it will not actually tell you what you should do. It will try to encourage you to make up your own mind in an informed and reasoned way and to act accordingly.

■ Understanding

In order to have a share in the communities to which we belong, we have to understand something of what is going on around us. If people are saying things that we don't understand, how can we join in?

Citizenship Studies should help you understand more about how society works and what it means to be a member of it.

■ Fairness and justice

A lot of the work you will do in Citizenship Studies will concern questions of fairness and justice.

These ideas are very important when discussing the ways in which people should be treated, or how society should be organised.

■ Participation

Using your rights and accepting your responsibilities is not always easy. Sometimes people don't know how to do this. Where do you go for information or help? How do you persuade someone that you are right? How do you give a person or an organisation useful and practical help?

Citizenship Studies will provide you with more confidence, skills and knowledge about how to become involved.

? question

1. Several people were asked what citizenship meant to them. Here are the answers that they gave:
   • 'having a vote and using it properly'
   • 'knowing your rights and sticking up for them'
   • 'looking after yourself and those around you'
   • 'doing something about the things that are wrong with society'
   • 'obeying the law and doing what's right.'

   Look at each of these statements and decide which ones you feel best describe what citizenship means to you. Explain the reasoning behind your answer.

   If you are not happy with any of the statements, what definition would you give instead?

About this book

help information

Purpose

This book is for use by both GCSE and non-GCSE students. It can be used as a resource to dip into for research, or as the main text to support your study in the GCSE (short course) in Citizenship Studies.

National Curriculum

The text covers all elements of the key stage 4 curriculum, including:

- rights, responsibilities and the law
- how our democratic system works
- community involvement
- social issues and current affairs.

The course will help you to understand how the society you live in works and your rights and responsibilities as a citizen. It will also help you to think about a range of interesting and controversial issues.

Exam

The book covers all elements of the OCR Citizenship Studies syllabus and has a final section that will:

- show you the structure and mark allocation for the exam
- outline what is expected in your course work
- indicate the differences between the three sections of the written paper and provide examples of typical questions and source materials.

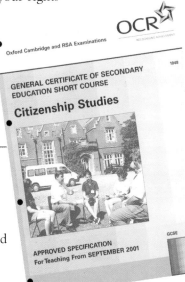

More than just a subject

The units in the book will provide the basis of the information you need to do well in the exam. However, you will almost certainly need further information and ideas through your own research using other books, the Internet, newspapers, television, and by making links with what you learn in other subjects.

Citizenship issues will occur in many of your subjects including English, geography, history, science and RE. Equally, what you learn in Citizenship Studies will help you to make your own sense of so much that is happening all around you.

It's the rule

In this unit we look at some of the characteristics and features of law.

Home time

Lauren got off the school bus and walked the short distance to her home. She lives with her dad and younger brother.

Lauren pressed the bell and waited on the doorstep. Her dad opened the door and, with a slightly annoyed expression, asked, 'Forgotten your key again?'

Lauren stepped inside and stood in the hall, still wearing her coat and holding her school bag. 'Hello,' she said.

'Aren't you going to take your coat off?' asked her dad.

'Oh, thank you,' said Lauren. 'Where shall I put it?'

'On the hook, of course,' her dad replied. 'Are you all right?'

'Yes thank you,' said Lauren, still standing in the hallway.

Her dad walked through to the kitchen. 'Cup of tea?' he called.

'Thank you very much,' answered Lauren. 'No sugar, please.'

'Lauren,' said her dad, beginning to look worried. 'What's the matter? You don't usually behave like this.'

? question

1. How is Lauren behaving? Is she behaving like a daughter, or someone else? What kind of person does her behaviour remind you of?

Rules

Although we don't always realise it, most – if not all – of our behaviour with other people follows certain rules. These rules vary from one group of people to another.

It is sometimes easiest to see the rules that we follow when they are broken. Lauren was breaking certain unwritten rules. She wasn't behaving like a daughter. She was behaving like a guest.

Relationships

One part of our lives closely controlled by rules is our relationships with other people. Take marriage, for example.

Here are some statements about marriage:
- **Age** Both partners must be aged 16 or over.
- **Faithful** A married person should not have a sexual relationship with someone else.
- **Sex** A couple should not have sex before they are married.
- **Support** When people are married they should behave reasonably towards each other and support each other.
- **Woman and man** The partners should be of the opposite sex.

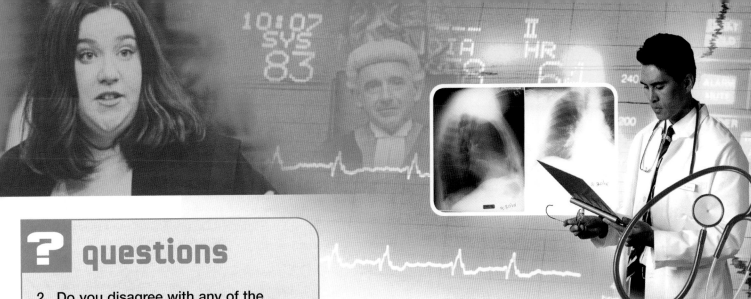

? questions

2. Do you disagree with any of the statements about marriage? Briefly explain why.

3. All the statements could be regarded as rules. Some of them are laws, and some are not. Which do you think are laws? What are the others?

Right and wrong

Many of the rules that we have in society are about questions of morality. That is, about what people believe is fundamentally right or wrong.

There are certain rules that most people generally agree with. Most believe it is wrong for a person to steal from others. This is something that is regarded as being morally wrong, and is also against the law.

Morality *v.* the law

Usually laws reflect the moral beliefs of most people in society, but this isn't *always* the case.

The case of Tony Bland In April 1989, Liverpool played Nottingham Forest in an FA Cup Semi-final at Hillsborough in Sheffield. Shortly before the match was due to start, a gate was opened on to one of the terraces, and fans streamed in to a section of the ground that was already very crowded.

In the crush that followed 96 people were killed. Among these was 17-year-old Tony Bland, who suffered serious damage to his brain, which rendered him unconscious, in what is known as a persistent vegetative state. His brain ceased to function in the normal way and, although he was able to breathe, doctors believed that he was unaware of anything that was happening around him.

Tony's family and doctors eventually decided that it would be better to allow Tony to die, rather than to continue to feed and treat him in his unconscious state. In 1992 an application was made to a court for permission to stop all of Tony's life-prolonging treatment.

In March 1993, the most senior judges in the country decided that it should not be against the law to remove the tube-delivered food and fluids, even though it would mean Tony would starve to death. Nine days later, he died.

The judges' decision, however, was very controversial. Some people felt that only God can decide when to end a life. Others argued that a law allowing doctors to discontinue maintaining a patient's life is open to abuse.

? question

4. Some people believe there are other things that people do that are morally wrong, and should be forbidden by law. Fox hunting, abortion and Sunday trading are examples of this.

   Select one of these, or choose an example of your own, and try to find out the arguments that people give for changing the law from its present state.

It's the rule

What is law?

■ On a wider scale

We have already seen that much of our life is affected by rules.

Rules made by our family or school usually just affect ourselves and the other people in these groups. If we come in late, don't put things away, or use the wrong entrance, we aren't normally breaking the law – just the rule of the group or organisation.

Laws are different. They are rules that apply in all situations, to everyone within the community – although there are some groups, such as children, who are not affected by some laws until they reach a certain age.

? questions

1. Legal rules influence many aspects of our lives. Look at each of the pictures above and draw up a list of some of the laws that apply to each situation shown.

2. Your list probably includes many different laws. Do they all perform the same kind of job or function? If not, what different functions do you think laws serve?

3. Now, either alone, or in pairs or small groups, try to draw a picture of what the law means to you. If you can, try not to use any words – just use symbols and pictures.

4. Compare the drawings of people in your class. What picture do people have of the law?

■ Positive or negative?

Many people have very negative views of the law. Ask people what they associate with law, and some will say words like expense, trouble and complicated. You may like to test this idea out yourself, with a small survey.

? questions

5. Can you suggest any reasons why people might have a negative view of the law?

6. Does it matter if some people distrust the law or feel defeated by it? What are the possible consequences of this for them and for others?

Civil and criminal law

One of the ways in which law can be divided up is into what is known as *civil* and *criminal* law.

Civil law provides a way of settling disputes between individuals or groups of people. When you buy something that fails to work, or doesn't do what the shop assistant claimed, it is the civil law that you use to get your money back. It's a mechanism for settling the disagreement between you and the shop.

Criminal law covers behaviour that the State has decided must be discouraged or prevented – such as assault or theft. These actions then become crimes. They are also usually dealt with by the police, or some other authority – and not by the individuals concerned.

A year in the life

Dear Chloe

I just thought I'd put this note in with the Christmas card to let you know some of our news over the past year – although, by the time you've finished reading it, you may wish that I hadn't bothered!

In January, Dean, who is now 18, passed his driving test. He bought a car soon afterwards, but already has a speeding conviction and two parking fines.

In April, Madeleine was caught shoplifting while she was supposed to be in school. She was arrested and taken to the police station. I hope it has taught her a lesson.

In July, my brother, who works on a farm, seriously injured his hand. The farmer had failed to replace the guard on a cutting blade. His union is helping him to get compensation.

In August, after 19 years of marriage, my divorce from John was finalised.

In September I had problems with a neighbour, who is refusing to cut down a tree that blocks most of our light – and in October, I lost my job. They said I was no longer up to standard. I'd worked there for ten years, with a perfect record. I am making a claim for unfair dismissal.

Since then, it's been very peaceful, although there was a sign that things were getting back to normal when my car was broken into last week and my new phone stolen. The sales assistant had said it was the perfect mobile. How right he was.

Much love,

Anna XX

? question

7. Write down all the law-related events that Anna lists in her letter opposite, and decide whether each one is part of the civil or criminal law.

The law machine

This unit explains where our laws come from and the ways in which they are made and changed.

Law makers

■ Development

The law that we have in England and Wales (laws in Northern Ireland and Scotland are sometimes different) has been created and developed in three main ways: by **Parliament**, by judges in court and through our links with Europe.

■ Parliament

Governments are responsible for deciding the nature of most new law. During a general election, all parties explain the policies that they will follow if elected. The winning party that forms the new government will then introduce a number of new laws, or changes in the existing law, in order to put its policies into practice. These are called statutes or Acts of Parliament.

Before the 2001 general election, the Labour Party promised to do more to stop offenders benefiting from crime. Labour won the election, and one of the **Bills** the new government put before Parliament was the *Proceeds of Crime Bill*. When this becomes law it will give increased powers to the courts to confiscate money gained through crimes such as drug dealing.

New laws may also be proposed by individual MPs through what is called a private members' Bill. However, the time for debating these Bills is very limited and only a small number succeed in becoming law.

Freedom of Information Act 2000

CHAPTER 36

Explanatory Notes have been produced to assist in the understanding of this Act and are available separately

The Abortion Act 1967 is an example of a private members' Bill that did become law – originally proposed by the then Liberal MP, David Steel.

■ Judge-made law

In the twelfth century, the King set up courts and appointed judges to travel around the country providing justice and sorting out disputes. Decisions made by these judges were written down, and have gradually been built up to form a detailed record of English law. This is called 'common law.'

Today, when a judge hears a case in court, lawyers tell the judge about any other cases where similar facts have been heard before. If they have, the judge will follow the decision established by senior or equal ranking judges in the earlier case.

Sometimes, however, senior judges feel that decisions made in the past do not fit in with the present-day thinking – and in these circumstances, they may reinterpret and change judge-made law, in line with this.

In 1991 a man was charged with rape after having sex with his wife against her will. His lawyers argued that he was not guilty because the law had said for many years that it was not rape if a husband forced his wife to have sex. Five senior judges disagreed. They said this was out of date and that the law should change. A man can now be found guilty of raping his wife.

▓ Europe

Never again   The Second World War, between 1939 and 1945, cost the lives of millions of people and caused huge destruction throughout Europe. In order to avoid another horrific war, many felt that it was important for the separate states in Europe to work much more closely together.

To try to achieve this, two important organisations were created, which have had a major impact on our law in Britain. These are the European Union (EU) and the Council of Europe.

European Union   The origins of the European Union go back to 1951 with a treaty between Belgium, France, Germany, Italy, Luxembourg and the Netherlands. Today the European Union has grown to a group of 15 nations, including the United Kingdom, with more countries hoping to join in the future.

In signing up to the Union, each member state agreed that European Union law would become part of its own national law – and, if they differed, that EU law would take priority.

Not all of our law is determined by the European Union, however. The main areas affected are employment, transport, agriculture, environment and trade.

The Council of Europe   Although many of the same countries belong to both the Council of Europe and the European Union, they are quite separate organisations.

The Council of Europe is concerned with human rights and international understanding, rather than economic matters, and one of its most important achievements has been the creation of the European Convention on Human Rights.

By signing the Convention in 1951, the British Government agreed that everyone in this country should enjoy the rights and freedoms set out in the Convention. In 2000, these rights became part of UK law when the *Human Rights Act* came into force. The Convention is looked at in more detail on page 19.

keywords

Bill
The text of a proposed new law, which must be approved by Parliament before becoming a statute or Act of Parliament.

Parliament
The main law-making body of the United Kingdom, consisting of the House of Commons, the House of Lords and the Crown.

The law machine

Parliamentary process

■ Government policy

The Government introduces most new Bills into Parliament in order to bring about changes in the law that it feels are important.

In the 1980s, the Conservative Government believed that trade unions were preventing many British industries from modernising and becoming more competitive. As a result, it passed a number of laws reducing their power.

■ Consultation

A great deal of discussion and consultation normally takes place before the wording of a Bill is drawn up. The Government talks to people who have knowledge of the area covered by the new law and will often issue what is called a Green Paper, setting out its main ideas for change. This is followed by a White Paper, with firmer proposals, which becomes the basis of the Bill debated in Parliament.

Members of the public are also able to give their views by letter or e-mail to their MP or to the government department concerned.

Trade union march – early 1980's

■ Pressure

Sometimes new laws are created as a result of public pressure.

In November 2000, the age of consent for male gay sex was lowered to 16, bringing it into line with the heterosexual age of consent. This was after a long campaign by many groups and individuals and a ruling by the **European Court of Human Rights**, which had said that discrimination of this kind broke the European Convention on Human Rights.

This meant that the British Government *had* to change the law in order to keep to the European Convention on Human Rights.

Getting down to detail Not all laws are discussed at great length. In order to save time, Parliament will sometimes give the relevant minister the power to determine the exact detail of the law. The law appears in what are known as *statutory instruments* or *regulations*. This process is known as secondary legislation.

Demonstration for gay rights, June 1998.

A Bill normally starts its passage through Parliament in the **House of Commons**, where it is debated by Members of Parliament (MPs).

First Reading

The Bill is introduced to Parliament. The title is read out and a date fixed for the Second Reading.

Second Reading

This is a debate, not on the detail, but on the general principles of the Bill.

The law was recently changed to provide people aged 75 and over with free TV licences. During the Second Reading of the Bill, MPs debated the strengths and weaknesses of this idea.

This is probably the most important stage of a Bill. Once a Bill has passed its Second Reading, there is a good chance that it will become law.

Committee Stage

A small group of MPs, or members of the House of Lords, now look at the Bill in close detail. They go through the wording line by line in order to check that it says exactly what is intended.

In theory this idea works well, but criticisms are made of the process.

After serving on a Committee one MP wrote that there was often very little discussion and a lot of pressure to work faster. 'We proposed our amendments,' he said, 'the Minister responded, and the amendment was usually voted down.

'Sometimes,' he went on, 'the Government actually agreed with the changes we were demanding, but couldn't be seen to be doing so. The answer was for us to drop our opposition and let the Government propose their own amendments, which were very similar to our own, and, hey presto, they're accepted.'

Report Stage and Third Reading

The Bill then moves back to the whole House where the Committee reports on the changes it has made.

The Report Stage is followed by the Third Reading, when the House of Commons takes a vote on the final version of the Bill.

The Bill is then passed to the **House of Lords**, where it is again discussed and examined in much the same way. Any changes that the House of Lords wishes to make are sent back the House of Commons for further consideration.

The Lords can delay a Bill for up to a year, but cannot prevent it becoming law.

Royal Assent

The Bill then goes to the Queen or King to be 'signed' – in practice this is just a formality. The Bill is then known as an Act of Parliament, and becomes law from whatever date is laid down.

keywords

European Court of Human Rights
A court that decides on cases in which it is claimed there has been a breach of the European Convention on Human Rights. It is situated in Strasbourg, in northeastern France.

House of Commons
The section of Parliament made up of elected MPs.

House of Lords
The section of Parliament that consists mainly of people who have been specially appointed as peers. Some people who are judges, senior bishops and who have inherited a title are also members.

15

The law machine

Judge-made law

WE HAVEN'T COME ACROSS *THIS* BEFORE!

Getting on line

Almost every company in Britain now has a website. Usually their web address is closely based on the name that they trade under – such as Cadbury or Kellogg's.

Anyone who wants their own website address can, on payment of a fee, register their chosen name with one of a number of organisations.

Some people, however, have gone one stage further and registered names that are not their own, which they believe will be useful – and profitable – to sell to others.

In the late 1990s a number of well-known British companies, including Marks & Spencer, Sainsbury's and Virgin, learnt that a group of dealers in Internet names had registered their companies' names without their agreement.

The dealers were hoping to sell the names back to the company or sell them on to someone else. Large sums of money could be involved. A chain of burger restaurants had been asked for £25,000 to buy back their name.

? question

1. Can you see anything wrong with this practice? Give reasons for your answer.

Off line? Marks & Spencer, and the other companies involved, believed that the names of the Internet addresses really belonged to them. They felt that it was wrong that they should have to pay a large amount of money for a name that they had used for many years. They also believed that their business and their reputation could be seriously damaged if the name was sold to someone else.

They decided to take their case to court to ask for their names to be handed back.

? question

2. Draw up a list of the points on either side of this argument. Who do you feel has the fairer case?

Problem We have already seen that, in reaching a verdict, judges must – where the facts are the same – follow the decisions made by senior judges in previous cases. This is known as a system of precedent.

The problem the judges faced on this occasion was that the Internet was a new development and courts had never heard a case of this kind before. There was no exact precedent or guidance on how this case should be judged.

Solution The judges decided that the evidence in Court showed that the dealers were deliberately trying to extract as much money as they could from companies like Marks & Spencer by threatening to sell these names to other people if the company did not pay up.

The dealers were ordered to give back the names to the companies on which they were based.

Judge-made law In reaching this decision, the judges in court created a new piece of law that will stand until it is overruled either by the decision of a higher court, or a new law passed by Parliament.

Precedent

The word *precede* means going before; and precedent is the name given to the system by which judges follow decisions made in previous cases, where the facts are the same.

If the decision of a court is challenged, the case will be taken to a higher court, normally the Court of Appeal. Here judges will apply decisions already made by the Court of Appeal or the House of Lords, which stands at the summit of the courts' structure. When the House of Lords is acting as a court of law, only the senior judges take part.

The House of Lords may follow its own past decisions or, when it appears right to do so, depart from this and create new law. This is called case law.

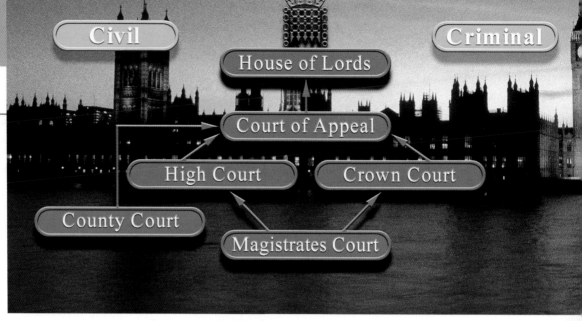

Civil

Criminal

House of Lords

Court of Appeal

High Court

Crown Court

County Court

Magistrates Court

Unelected lawmakers

In the United States, many judges are elected by local communities. In England and Wales they are experienced lawyers appointed by the Queen or King on the advice of the Lord Chancellor – a senior lawyer appointed by the Prime Minister and also a member of the Government.

In England and Wales almost all senior judges are men. At the time of writing, two out of 33 judges who work in the Court of Appeal are women. There are no women judges in the House of Lords.

There are no black or Asian judges working in the High Court, the Court of Appeal or the House of Lords.

Most judges were educated in fee-paying schools. Statistics are not published about their age, but it is probably fair to assume that very few are below 50 years of age.

? question

3. Try to explain the advantages of developing the law through a system of case law. Can you think of any disadvantages? If so, what are they?

? questions

4. Does it matter if judges are drawn from a small section of the community? Give reasons for your view.

5. Some people are concerned that judges are not sufficiently in touch with ordinary people. The Lord Chancellor has said he wants to change this. What suggestions could you make to ensure that judges have more understanding of the lives of people in Britain?

The law machine

Human rights law

On 1 September 1939 the people of Warsaw experienced their first air raid from German bombers. These were repeated every day for the next 27 days, until the city finally fell.

On 25 September blanket aerial bombing by 400 German warplanes set whole streets on fire. About 12,000 people were killed in these raids.

On 15 October the German army ordered that all Jewish people should be moved to a district in the north-western part of the city. Around 400,000 people were crowded together. By 1942 100,000 had died from starvation and disease.

On 22 July 1942 the planned extermination of Warsaw's Jewish population began. By 12 September 310,322 men, women and children had been sent to death camps and gassed.

On 19 April 1943 the German army tried to liquidate the Jewish quarter by setting fire to all the buildings. On 16 May Hitler was told that the district had ceased to exist.

■ The United Nations and the Universal Declaration of Human Rights

United Nations peacekeepers in Sierra Leone, West Africa.

During the Second World War, the inhabitants of almost every country in the world suffered the effects of war. It is estimated that 50 million people died as a result of the conflict.

Immediately after the end of the War in 1945, anxious not to repeat the mistakes of the past, 51 countries came together to form the United Nations. Today, it is an international organisation to which most countries of the world now belong, which works to try to prevent war and to maintain international peace and security.

In 1948 the United Nations drew up the *Universal Declaration of Human Rights*, setting out basic human rights to which, it was agreed, everyone is entitled.

Rights listed in the *Declaration* include:
- protection from arbitrary arrest
- the right to a fair trial
- freedom of thought, conscience and religion
- freedom of peaceful assembly
- the right to education.

It is important to note that the *Universal Declaration of Human Rights* does not have the force of law but is, nevertheless, a very important measure by which the behaviour of states can be judged.

UN Human Rights Commission

The United Nations Human Rights Commission investigates cases where governments are suspected of abusing people's human rights. If there is evidence that a serious breach of human rights has taken place an attempt will be made to put the suspect on trial at an International Criminal Tribunal in the Hague in Holland.

A well-known example of this is the case of Slobodan Milosevic, the former Yugoslav leader.

Former Yugoslav President, Slobodan Milosevic

■ European Convention on Human Rights

Like the *UN Declaration*, the *European Convention on Human Rights* was written shortly after the War and is designed to ensure the protection of basic human rights. Most of the rights it includes are set out on pages 22–23.

There is, however, a major difference between the *European Convention* and the *UN Declaration*, which is that the *Convention* offers a way for governments or individuals to enforce the rights that it contains.

Anyone who feels that their rights under the *Convention* have been broken may take their case to the European Court of Human Rights in Strasbourg, France. If the Court finds that the *Convention* has been broken, it can award damages to the person who brought the case and the country involved will almost certainly be required to change its law to ensure that it no longer breaks the *Convention*. This has happened several times to Britain.

Corporal punishment in school In September 1976, Jeffrey Cosans, then aged 15, took a short cut through a cemetery on his way home from school. This was against the rules, and Jeffrey was reported to the headteacher. The head decided to punish Jeffrey with the strap – but the boy refused. Jeffrey's parents supported him. They believed that corporal punishment was wrong. Jeffrey was suspended from school.

Eventually the head teacher and local authority said that Jeffrey could come back to school – but could not promise his parents that Jeffrey would not be beaten if he misbehaved again. Jeffrey did not return. Four months later he passed the school leaving age, and officially left.

Jeffrey's mother believed that the actions of the school and the local authority had broken the *European Convention on Human Rights*, and decided to take their case to the European Court of Human Rights.

The Court agreed, and found that the United Kingdom had broken the *European Convention* by not respecting the parents' objections to corporal punishment.

After this judgement, the British government had to change the law, in order not to break the *Convention*. In 1987 corporal punishment was abolished in state schools, and in all private schools in 1999.

? questions

1. What examples can you give of ways in which governments have failed to respect people's human rights?

2. What are the arguments in favour of having international agreements that are designed to protect human rights?

   Can you think of any difficulties that might be associated with these agreements?

3. Look at the rights listed in the *European Convention* on pages 22–23. Are there any other rights that you think might be included?

Human Rights Act 1998

The long route

The United Kingdom was the first country to sign the *European Convention on Human Rights*. However, almost every government we have had since 1953 has been reluctant to make the *Convention* part of our law, believing that doing so would interfere with Parliament's right to decide the law.

One consequence of this was that anyone who wanted to try to enforce a right under the *Convention* could do so only by taking their case to the European Court of Human Rights in Strasbourg. This could be a very long and difficult process. One case took nine years to progress through the system.

All change

After winning in the 1997 general election, the Labour Party began to put in practice their promise to incorporate the *Convention* into UK law, and in 1998 the *Human Rights Act* was passed by Parliament. It became law in 2000.

Almost all the rights in the *European Convention* are now part of UK law. These rights are listed on pages 22–23. But what does this actually mean? What difference does the Act make to our legal system?

All laws Under the *Human Rights Act* all our laws must, so far as is possible, be compatible with the Act. This means that any laws we have that are not in line with the *Convention* must be changed, and all new law must follow the terms of the *Convention*.

The only time in which this is not necessary is in very special circumstances, such as war or other national emergencies.

Courts When a judge in a British court makes a decision about a case, he or she must follow the principles of the *Convention* and take into account decisions already made by the European Court of Human Rights.

Public authorities

A final important feature of the *Human Rights Act* is the requirement for all public bodies – such as local authorities, hospitals, schools, and the police – to carry out their work in a way that upholds the rights that have been taken from the *Convention*. If they don't, then the body – the hospital or the police – may be challenged in court.

Terrorism Article 15 of the *Convention* allows countries to release themselves from their duties under the *Convention* in times of emergency – if it is felt to be absolutely essential. This is called derogation. The United Kingdom has taken up this option to hold or to deport people whom it regards as a terrorist threat.

Getting the right balance

Details of those parts of the *European Convention on Human Rights* that have been incorporated into the *Human Rights Act* are given on pages 22–23.

Some of the rights are absolute and cannot be interfered with by the State. These are contained in Articles 2, 3, 4, 7 and 14. For example, torture (Article 3) is not acceptable under any circumstances.

However, the rights contained in Articles 8, 9, 10 and 11 in particular, may in some circumstances be restricted – for reasons of public safety or to protect the rights of others.

In situations such as these, a court must decide whether it is reasonable to restrict a person's right in some way. Usually this involves balancing two competing rights.

For example in 2001, the High Court had to decide whether newspapers could report the whereabouts of the two boys who murdered toddler Jamie Bulger after they had served their sentence and been released from prison.

On the one hand, it was argued that newspapers had the right to publicise this information. On the other, it was argued that the boys would face the risk of death or serious injury if their addresses were revealed. Here the right to freedom of expression (Article 10) is competing with the right to life (Article 2).

? questions

1. In what situations do you think it would be reasonable to limit a person's right to a) free speech, b) meet or gather with whoever they wish? Explain why.

2. Look at the example on the right and decide what you think are the two rights that are in question. What kind of judgement would you give in a case like this? Give reasons for your answer.

A right to privacy In 2001 the *Daily Mirror* newspaper published a photograph and details of the model Naomi Campbell attending a meeting of Narcotics Anonymous – a support group to help drug addicts recover from their habit.

Naomi Campbell said that the paper had no right to print information about such a personal problem. She said that the publicity from the article made her depressed and miserable.

The newspaper said that because Ms Campbell's career depended on publicity, she lost her right to privacy. It also added that Ms Campbell had on a previous occasion said that she did not take drugs. This was untrue.

The European Convention on Human Rights

The following sections of the European Convention on Human Rights are included in the Human Rights Act 1998.

The European Convention on Human Rights

Article 2
Right to life
Everyone has the right to have their life protected by law. Taking a life is acceptable only when it is absolutely necessary, such as in self-defence or to protect the life of someone else.

Article 3
Prohibition of torture
Everyone has the right to be free from torture and inhuman or degrading punishment.

Article 4
Prohibition of slavery and forced labour
No one shall be held in slavery or required to perform forced labour. This right does not apply to work related to military, prison or community service.

Article 5
Right to liberty and security
Everyone has the right not to be detained and deprived of their liberty, unless it is within the law and the correct legal procedures followed.

Article 6
Right to a fair trial
Everyone has the right to a fair trial and a public hearing within a reasonable period of time. Everyone charged with a criminal offence shall be presumed innocent until proved guilty.

Article 7
No punishment without law
No one should be found guilty of an offence that was not a crime at the time it took place. Nor should they receive a heavier punishment than was applicable when the offence was committed.

The European Convention on Human Rights

Article 8
Right to respect for a person's private and family life
Everyone has the right to respect for their private and family life, their home, and their correspondence.

Article 9
Freedom of thought, conscience, and religion
Everyone is free to hold whatever views and beliefs they wish – but their right to express their views can be restricted in certain circumstances.

Article 10
Freedom of expression
Everyone has the right of freedom to express their opinion – but this may be limited for reasons, for example of public safety and to protect the rights of others.

Article 11
Freedom of assembly and association
Everyone has the right to get together with other people in a peaceful way, this includes the right to form and join a trade union.

Article 12
Right to marry
Men and women have the right to marry and have a family – but are bound by the laws covering whom people may or may not marry and where a marriage may take place.

Article 14
Prohibition of discrimination
Everyone is entitled to the rights and freedoms set out in the *Convention* regardless of their race, sex, language, religion, political opinion, national or social origin, birth or other status.

The rights listed in Articles 8–11 are not absolute, but may be restricted in order to protect things like public safety or the rights of others, or to prevent crime. Someone who feels that a right has been restricted unfairly may complain to a Court, which will decide whether it is reasonable.

A number of further points were added to the Convention at a later date. These are known as protocols.

Convention on Human Rights

Article 2
Right to education
No one shall be denied the right to education. The State must respect the right of parents to ensure that their child's education follows their own religious and philosophical beliefs.

Article 3
Right to free elections
Elections for government must be free and fair and must take place by secret ballot.

Protocol 1 Article 1
Protection of property
No one shall be deprived of their possessions, except in very limited circumstances. These allow, for example, the State to take money for the payment of taxes or confiscate goods which are unlawful or pose some kind of danger.

Protocol 6 Articles 1 & 2
Abolition of the death penalty
No one shall be condemned to death or executed. However, a state may make provision for the death penalty in its law at times of war or imminent threat of war.

Consumer rights

This unit outlines the law covering many of the things that we buy every day.

Contract

Not necessarily in writing

Almost every time we buy **goods** or **services** we enter into a contract.

This is a legal agreement in which a person, a company, or some kind of organisation agrees to provide goods or a service for someone else in return, usually, for money.

Contracts, as everyone knows, can be long and complicated documents. But most of the contracts that we make are not written down at all. Every time we buy something from a shop, a contract is made between the shop owner and ourselves.

A contract can also be made, even if nothing is said between the people involved. Paying for parking in a ticket machine or buying goods on the Internet are examples of this.

Failing to deliver

If the thing that you have paid for doesn't work properly or is not what you were promised, it means that the shop or person you were dealing with has failed to keep their side of the contract.

In this situation the law says that you are entitled to your money back or **compensation** from the person or company with whom the contract was made.

? question

1. Look at the pictures above and decide, in each case, whether a contract has been broken and, if so, by whom.

What if......?

A
- the customer complains that the coffee is cold?
- the customer decides she would rather have tea?

B
- the customer buys the PC, but later decides that she can't afford it?
- the customer has to wait much longer for the computer to be delivered that she expected?

C
- the customer wishes to change the carton of orange juice for a cheaper brand?

- the checkout assistant realises that a jar of drinking chocolate has been wrongly priced? She tells the customer she will have to pay £2 more.

■ Disappointment

Elaine and Gary booked their honeymoon in the seaside resort of Sosua in the Dominican Republic. The tour operator's brochure promised that everything was included in the price.

'Every single gin and tonic, every single snack and nightcap has been paid in advance,' claimed the brochure.

'All leisure facilities, like archery, scuba diving and the health suite are completely free of charge.'

But when Elaine and Gary reached the hotel, the service that they received was not what they had expected.

'Just after we arrived,' Elaine explained, 'we were given a photocopied list of everything that was free. The trouble was, it just didn't match the brochure.'

Gary explained that they both planned to learn how to scuba dive when they were out there. 'The first lesson, in the swimming pool, was free,' said Gary, 'but after that it cost £30 an hour and you had to take a bus further up the coast, because it was too dangerous to swim in the water where we were.'

'We really felt cheated,' said Elaine. 'Our choice of free alcoholic drinks was limited to four – and you had to pay for anything you wanted to drink after eleven o'clock at night.'

'Sosua itself was lovely,' said Gary, 'but we felt we had been misled. There were no archery facilities at all – and the health suite was little more than a couple of cycling machines and a sun lounger. We've got one of those at home.

'The fortnight's holiday cost £2,500 – and I reckon we had to pay another £400 just to do the things that we had planned.

'We weren't the only ones who were disappointed. Other people at the hotel felt the same way. In fact when we complained to the manager, he said that the holiday that we had booked had been withdrawn in December – but that the tour operator was still continuing to offer it.'

? questions

2. Why were Elaine and Gary disappointed with their holiday?

3. Who was responsible for the holiday not being as they expected?

4. After their holiday Elaine and Gary wrote to the tour operator to complain about the problems that they had on their holiday.

   Look at the rest of the information on this double-page spread. What points would you suggest Elaine and Gary should make in their letter to the tour operator?

keywords

Compensation
A sum of money to make up for loss or damage a person suffers.

Goods
Items or possessions.

Services
Work that is done for payment, such as hairdressing, plumbing or repairs to a car.

Consumer rights

When things go wrong

■ As we were

For hundreds of years there have been laws designed to protect the quality and price of things that ordinary people buy. The sale of essential items, such as bread, beer, meat and fuel, has almost always been controlled by law.

However, anyone buying something else – like a horse or a cart – had very little protection in law. If the horse was sick or the cart fell to pieces, there was little a buyer could do, unless they could prove that they had been *deliberately* misled at the time of purchase. This is the origin of the legal expression *caveat emptor*, meaning *buyer beware*. It is still used today, and is particularly important when buying something privately, such as a car.

Best before In 1350, Londoner Richard Quelhogge bought, for four pence, a pig that he found lying by the side of the Thames. Richard then apparently cut off the hind legs of the animal and tried to sell them.

Whether they were bought and eaten is not known, but Richard did find himself in court for selling *putride and stinking meat*. He was found guilty and sentenced to stand in the pillory, whilst the remainder of the animal was burnt at his feet.

■ Changing times

The end of the nineteenth century was a time of great change in Britain. Many people left the countryside and moved into towns and cities and more and more of the goods they used were made in factories. But when these items didn't work or failed in some way, it was very difficult for people to get their money back or obtain compensation.

One problem was the law. There were no neat rules, setting out people's rights and responsibilities. Instead, the law lay hidden in complicated documents, recording verdicts brought by judges in court.

In order to deal with this, Parliament in the late 1800s passed a whole new series of Acts. These tried to set out the law relating to goods and services in a much clearer and simpler way.

Today

During the twentieth century the law continued to change as shopping and buying things grew in importance in our society.

The law applying to most of the things that we buy today is the *Sale of Goods Act 1979*. This states that all goods sold by a trader must be:

✓ *of satisfactory quality* They must be free from faults and not scratched or damaged in any way.

✓ *fit for their purpose* The goods must do what they are designed to do and, in particular, what the sales assistant or the packaging claims.

✓ *as described* They must be the same as they are described in an advertisement, on the packaging or by the sales assistant.

Goods bought privately, for example from a neighbour or through an advert in the local paper, must only be *as described*.

Problems Complaints about faulty goods should be made to the place from which they were bought. The contract is with the shop, not the manufacturer.

When faulty goods are returned, the customer has the right to have their money back in full.

Time There is no set time limit in which goods must be returned if they are faulty, but it is important to tell the seller about the problem as soon as possible.

For example, someone who buys a personal stereo, and finds when they get home that it doesn't work properly, has a right to reject the goods and get their money back.

If they use the stereo, knowing that it is faulty, or do not complain within a reasonable time, they are seen, in law, to have accepted the goods – and this makes it much harder to claim a refund.

IS IT TOO LATE TO RETURN THIS?

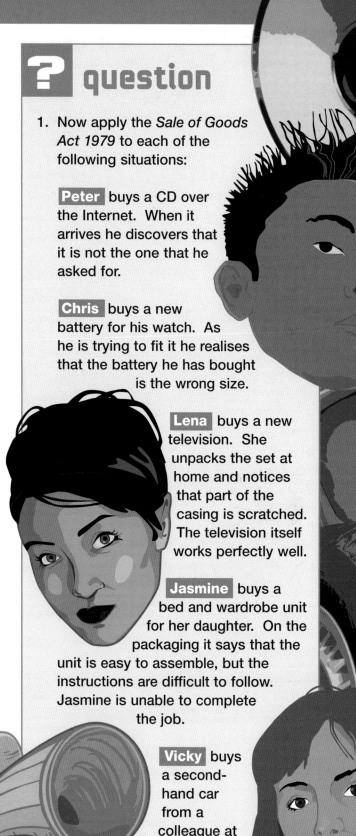

? question

1. Now apply the *Sale of Goods Act 1979* to each of the following situations:

Peter buys a CD over the Internet. When it arrives he discovers that it is not the one that he asked for.

Chris buys a new battery for his watch. As he is trying to fit it he realises that the battery he has bought is the wrong size.

Lena buys a new television. She unpacks the set at home and notices that part of the casing is scratched. The television itself works perfectly well.

Jasmine buys a bed and wardrobe unit for her daughter. On the packaging it says that the unit is easy to assemble, but the instructions are difficult to follow. Jasmine is unable to complete the job.

Vicky buys a second-hand car from a colleague at work. A week later, a major fault appears, costing £480 to repair.

27

Consumer wrongs

It is an offence for shops to sell dangerous goods or deliberately to mislead their customers. This unit explains some of the criminal aspects of consumer law.

Mott the who?

Phil is a keen fan of the 1970s pop group Mott the Hoople and was interested to see advertised, in a music magazine, a new compilation CD of their greatest hits.

When the CD arrived, Phil sat down to listen to it, but soon realised that neither the backing band nor the singers were the real Mott the Hoople.

Phil decided to inform the group's management, who then got in touch with the local **trading standards department**.

The record company had bought the recordings from someone who claimed that they were made by the original band. 'It did not occur to us,' the company said, 'that they would not be genuine.'

The CD bought by Phil was not *as described*, and so – under the *Sale of Goods Act 1979* – he was entitled to his money back from the mail-order firm from whom he bought the record.

▨ A criminal offence

In falsely describing the CD as Mott the Hoople's own recordings, the record company had also committed a criminal offence.

As a result, the company was taken to court and charged, under the *Trade Descriptions Act 1968*, of supplying a CD with a false description. It was fined £8,000.

? question

1. Why is falsely describing something for sale a *criminal* offence?

Dangerous goods

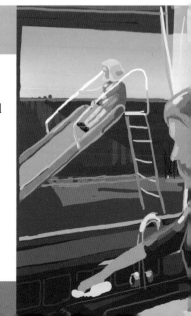

People have a right to expect that the things they buy are safe and are not dangerous to use. It's a criminal offence to sell something that is either dangerous or is not up to the safety standards required by law.

▨ A tragic accident

Chloe, aged 3, was playing on a children's slide in the garden at home when her head became trapped between the top of the slide and a metal support.

Her mother found her hanging from the slide and, despite being rushed to hospital, Chloe died six days later.

An investigation into the accident was held, and the company that made and sold the slide was charged with selling an unsafe toy.

Evidence Here are some of the facts and statements that were given at the trial.

A The company had made and sold 200,000 slides before this before this accident occurred

B As soon as they heard about Chloe's accident the company withdrew the slide from sale. Sixteen days later it was on sale again with safety modifications.

C/ In the opinion of a safety experts, the design of the design of the slide meets current British safety standards.

D) A director of the company stated, 'This slide has an excellent safety record. We have never had a serious accident or a death with any of our products.'

(E) Chloe's mother explained, 'I had been with Chloe in the garden, watching her playing on the slide. I then went into the house. After a while I realised that I couldn't hear her. I looked out of the window and saw Chloe hanging from the slide'.

F - The company now offers a special safety kit for those people who bought the slide before the accident.

G - A safety expert said, 'It is not always possible to predict what young children will do'.

H - Another senior company director said, ' These slides are used in our stores. About two million children a year use them under staff supervision.

? questions

2. In court, the judge had to decide whether the company was guilty of selling an unsafe toy.

   Some of the evidence heard in the court is listed on the left. Which items would help the judge to decide whether the company had or had not broken the law?

3. Now choose the four or five pieces of evidence that you feel are most important in this case. Explain why you feel each one that you have selected is important.

4. Would you find the toy company guilty or not guilty of selling an unsafe toy?

5. If you feel the toy company is guilty, what punishment would you impose? The maximum fine for this offence is £5,000.

❖ keywords

Trading standards department
People employed by the local authority to check that local shops and businesses are not breaking the law in the way that they trade. If they believe that an offence has been committed they can prosecute the trader.

Consumer complaints

In this unit we look at ways of making a complaint and successfully dealing with problems of faulty goods and services.

Taking action

■ Washed up

Therese O'Dell bought an expensive new washing machine. But, after six months' use, it broke down. Mrs O'Dell rang the shop where she bought it and was told to call the manufacturer's help line. This she did. They said an engineer would come to her house to look at her machine.

The engineer didn't arrive. Nor did he keep a second appointment. It took three weeks for someone to come. Then they left – saying that new parts were needed before the machine could be repaired.

A week later the parts were installed. But the washing machine soon broke down again.

Another call to the engineer, and another week passed before anyone appeared. The engineer told Mrs O'Dell that the same parts needed replacing and would take a further week to be delivered.

? questions

1. Draw up a list of the difficulties that Mrs O'Dell is facing because of the problem with her washing machine.

2. What do you think is the greatest difficulty she faces in getting someone to deal with the problem?

3. What should Mrs O'Dell do next? Draw up a list of actions that she could take. Put them in order of effectiveness. Which would you recommend?

Problems

The difficulties that people face when the goods or services that they have bought go wrong are rarely straightforward.

? question

4. All the cases opposite are based on real life. Using the information on pages 32–33, put yourself in the position of someone who has been asked to give advice.

In each case a) outline the person's position in law, and b) suggest what action they should take.

Sairah This year I went to India for my holiday. The day after I got home I took four films in for developing. When I went to collect them they told me that two of the films had been lost – and offered me just under £10 – the cost of replacing the film.

I said that this was not enough – but they pointed to the small print on my receipt which says that if the film is damaged or lost then the company will only pay the replacement cost of the film.

Alex I bought a video recorder from a shop in town. The assistant said the price was reduced because it was a discontinued model. When I unpacked the recorder at home I found that the instruction booklet had been used and someone else's TV licence was inside the box!

Louisa Last night my 12-year-old son was eating a piece of bread pudding when he found a screw in his mouth. I'd bought the pudding in the afternoon from the local supermarket. It cost me £1.79.

Adam I bought a new computer package, with a printer, for £1,300. The sales assistant said it would be able to print up to eight pages a minute. In fact it sometimes takes five minutes to do a single page.

I rang the company's help line but got fed up waiting for someone to talk to, so I rang the printer manufacturer. They said that I'd been sold the wrong printer for my computer. The right one will cost me £140.

The company I bought the package from refuse to help. They won't take the old printer because it has been used and cannot be resold.

Clive I bought my car through an advert in the local paper. The man said it was a good runner and I paid him £4,200. It was fine for the first couple of weeks – now I've discovered it needs a new clutch and gearbox, which will cost about £1,000. I've written to ask him for £500 – which I thought was fair – but he's ignored my letter.

Yvonne I ordered a new bath. The shop said it would cost £340, which I agreed to. This week they called to say that the factory had put its prices up. If I want the bath I will have to pay another £120.

✳ coursework idea

Find an example of a complaint that someone has made over a product or a service that they have bought. This may be based on your own experience or that of someone else.

Outline the nature of the complaint and the arguments and actions of both sides. How was the problem settled?

What were the difficulties faced by each side in the dispute. Was one in a more powerful position than the other? Explain.

Consumer complaints

Problem solving – a guide

First things

Take it back Many shops will exchange faulty goods immediately, as long as the customer has a receipt or some other proof of purchase.

Ask to see the manager Sometimes it helps to ask to see a more senior person, such as the manager or supervisor.

Write a letter A letter to the company head office is often the next stage, with the customer explaining why they are dissatisfied with what they have bought.

Keep a record If the matter is not settled immediately, it's a good idea for the customer to keep a note of everything they have done, as well as copies of letters sent and received.

Finding help

Citizens Advice Bureaux These are advice centres, usually known as CABs, which give free help and guidance about all kinds of problems. There are offices in most towns and cities. The telephone number is in the local phone book.

Small claims procedure Anyone over 18 unable to get satisfaction over a problem with faulty goods or poor service can try to recover their money by putting their case to a judge in a county court.

The court is very informal and there is no need to employ a lawyer. It is a relatively simple and inexpensive way of settling a case, up to the value of £5,000.

Solicitors These are trained lawyers able to give advice and take action on behalf of their clients over a range of legal issues. With consumer problems, however, there is a danger that the cost of the solicitor's fees will be greater than the value of the goods concerned.

McFadden & Taylor

Trading standards departments Sometimes known as consumer protection departments, these give advice to the public about all kinds of consumer problems. However, their main job is to check that shops and traders keep within the law and they will prosecute if there is evidence that the trader has committed a criminal offence.

citizens advice bureau

■ The law

Sale of Goods Act 1979 This states that all goods sold by a trader must be:

- *of satisfactory quality:* They must be free from faults and not scratched or damaged in any way.
- *fit for their purpose:* The goods must do what they are designed to do and, in particular, what the sales assistant or the packaging claims.
- *as described:* They must be the same as they are described in an advertisement, on the packaging or by the sales assistant.

Goods bought privately must be only *as described*.

Supply of Goods and Services Act 1982
This states that a service must be provided:

- with reasonable care and skill
- within a reasonable time, and
- at a reasonable cost, if no price has been agreed in advance.

Consumer Credit Act 1984 If there's a fault with something bought using a credit card, the customer may be able to claim from the credit card company as well as the firm from which the goods were bought.

This applies only to goods costing more than £100, but can be useful if the trader is being unhelpful or is no longer in business.

Unfair Contract Terms Act 1977 The wording or small print of a customer's contract must be fair. If it is not, the customer can ask a court to overturn it.

For example, a security firm that fitted alarms had a section in its contract that said they would not be responsible if their alarm failed and the customer's house was burgled. This, a court decided, was unfair. The customer was paid compensation and the company forced to change its contracts.

Trade Descriptions Act 1968
It is a criminal offence for a trader to make a deliberately misleading or false claim about what they are selling.

> IT DOES *WHAT* IT SAYS ON THE TIN!

Consumer Safety Act 1987 It is a criminal offence for a trader to sell goods that are not safe. The law applies to both new and second-hand goods, unless the buyer was specifically told that they were faulty or in need of repair.

Anyone suffering injury or damage from unsafe or dangerous goods can claim damages from the manufacturer.

Looking for work

This unit looks at the rights and responsibilities that employers and employees have at work.

On the move

Almost everyone living in Britain today has their origins elsewhere. We are a nation of **migrants** – able to trace our roots to countries in all parts of Europe, the Middle East, Africa, Asia and the Caribbean.

Romans, Saxons, Vikings and Normans came to Britain to invade and conquer. Others, particularly from Africa, were brought by force as slaves and servants. Refugees from France, Germany, Russia and other parts of Europe came to Britain to escape persecution and violence in their own country.

A better life

The other reason for many people coming to Britain has been the hope that they, or their children, would find a better standard of living here than in the country that they had left.

Economic migration, as this is called, goes back a long way. Records show that people from France, Germany, Italy and Holland were settling in London and elsewhere for this reason as early as 1130AD.

Skills

Many migrants bring useful skills. The merchants who came from France in the twelfth century brought an understanding of money and trade that was unfamiliar to the British – and were the founders of London's banking and financial services.

From the fourteenth century, other trades – connected with weaving, printing, brewing and engineering – were brought by the French, Germans and Dutch.

Filling a gap

Migrants often move to countries where there is a shortage of labour or where it is difficult to get people to do certain jobs.

At the end of the Second World War in 1945, there was the huge task of rebuilding Britain, damaged by six years of war.

As there were not enough people available for work, the British government started to encourage workers from other parts of Europe to help with this process of reconstruction. A year later, in 1948, the invitation was extended to people in Ireland and the West Indies.

Some industries launched large advertising campaigns to attract workers to Britain. London Transport set up centres in the West Indies to recruit bus crews, and textile and engineering firms in the north of England and Midlands sent agents to find workers in India and Pakistan.

For about 25 years, people from the West Indies, India, Pakistan, and later Bangladesh, travelled to work and settle in Britain.

Arriving from Jamaica, June 1948

Clinton Edwards I joined the RAF and came over to England in 1942, and was in the War for three years. When I went back to Jamaica there was no work. So I decided to return to England where the opportunity for jobs was better than back home.

Sher Azan I came to Britain from Pakistan in 1961, when I was 20. My father was against it, but I managed to persuade him that there were better employment opportunities over here. In fact, British companies placed advertisements for work in our local newspaper.

■ Two-way traffic

Britain has also been a country that many people have *left*. From the seventeenth to the twentieth centuries, large numbers of people departed from Britain to settle in parts of Africa, the United States, Canada, Australia and New Zealand. In the 50 years between 1850 and 1900, five and a half million people emigrated from England, Scotland and Wales.

EMIGRATION TO NEW ZEALAND PARADISE

Every industrious young man or woman in good health will, on approval, receive a **FREE GIFT** *of Forty Acres of Good Land in the province of Auckland, New Zealand, together with Forty Acres more for each person above 18 years* **AND** *Twenty Acres for each child above five.*

■ The importance of the Commonwealth

The British Empire once included much of Africa, Canada, the Indian sub-continent and Australasia.

Since 1945, almost all these countries have become independent and together now form an association called the Commonwealth, with the Queen as its head.

A common language and similarities in culture have greatly assisted the movement of people, and Commonwealth links have had a major effect on migration to and from Britain.

Membership of both the Commonwealth and the European Union sometimes brings difficulties for Britain in deciding the best course of action over matters like trading loyalties and immigration.

? questions

1. There is a strong possibility that you and other students in your class will spend part of your working life in another country. If you had the opportunity to move, which country or countries would you choose? What would be the reasons for your choice?

2. What difficulties do you imagine that you might face? How could you try to overcome them?

3. Who would have responsibility for your safety and well-being in the country where you were working?

✦ keyword

Migrant
Someone moving from one place or country to another. Emigrant describes a person who leaves their region or country. Immigrant refers to a person arriving from another region or country.

Looking for work

Race discrimination

■ Prejudice

Suzanne Jones, a black English woman, applied for a job as a clerical assistant at a firm of solicitors. She was 19 and well qualified for the post. But, after an interview with Mr Wheeler, the senior partner, she was not offered the job.

Six weeks later, Suzanne saw an advertisement for a similar job at the same firm. She phoned to say she was interested, and realised that she was speaking to the same Mr Wheeler whom she had previously met.

Suzanne was again invited for interview, but when she walked into Mr Wheeler's office he recognised her and became very upset. He did not even ask her to sit down, saying that there was no point in going ahead with the interview. He asked Suzanne to leave.

Suzanne believed that she was being rejected because of the colour of her skin. She told Mr Wheeler that she had no wish to work for him, called him a bigot – and left.

Later that day, Mr Wheeler interviewed another applicant, Deborah Cook, who was white. During the course of the interview Mr Wheeler said to Deborah, 'A coloured girl applied for the job – but why would I want to take her on, when English girls are available?'

Deborah was offered the job, but turned it down. Instead she decided to tell someone in the local race relations office what Mr Wheeler had said.

■ Advice

Suzanne knew that racial discrimination was against the law and went to see a solicitor to seek advice – but not one who worked for Mr Wheeler's firm. The solicitor told Suzanne that she believed that Mr Wheeler had broken the *Race Relations Act* and that

Suzanne was entitled to take her case to an **employment tribunal**. If the tribunal decided that Mr Wheeler had acted in an unlawful way, Suzanne would be entitled to **compensation**.

■ Tribunal

Mr Wheeler told the tribunal that he hadn't unfairly discriminated against Suzanne. She failed to get the job, he said, because she was rude and not sufficiently qualified.

? question

1. Put yourself in the position of someone listening to this case. Does the evidence suggest that Suzanne was a victim of racial discrimination or has Mr Wheeler shown that he acted fairly? What would be your decision, and why?

■ Yesterday and today

In the 1950s and 1960s some people feared that those coming from the Caribbean, India and Pakistan posed a threat to their jobs and housing. Although this was a period of full employment, with not enough people to fill the jobs available, black people still faced considerable discrimination. It was not uncommon to see signs saying *Rooms to let – no coloureds*.

Racial discrimination of this kind, in employment and housing, became illegal in 1976.

▓ No joke

Trevor McCauley, from Antrim in Northern Ireland, had worked in England for 20 years. During this time he heard more than his fair share of jokes about the Irish. Over the last two years, however, working at a firm in Derbyshire, he was on the receiving end of critical comments almost continuously.

'Every day,' he said, 'they were saying things like "typical thick Paddy" and "what else can you expect from an Irishman".

'I decided that I had had enough. When I started to complain, they told me I had an attitude problem.

'I was harassed every day. You feel absolutely useless. Eventually I got the sack for being a troublemaker.'

An employment tribunal decided that anti-Irish remarks amounted to racial discrimination and that Mr McCauley had been unfairly dismissed from work. He received an award of £6,000 in compensation.

❓ questions

2. Racial discrimination is something that affects thousands of people's lives. It makes them afraid. It makes them angry. It damages their confidence.

   What do you think makes people racially **prejudiced**? Draw up a list of possible explanations.

3. Is it right to have a law banning racial discrimination at work? Give reasons for your answer.

▓ The law

Under the *Race Relations Act 1976* it is against the law for an employer to treat a person less favourably because of their race, colour, nationality or ethnic origin.

Race discrimination is not unlawful if the employment is in a private household.

❖ keywords

Compensation
A sum of money to compensate, or make up, for the loss that a person has suffered.

Employment tribunal
A court of law that decides on employment disputes such as discrimination and unfair dismissal. Cases are heard by a panel of three people – a lawyer, and two others from work and industry. One of these will be from an employer's organisation, the other from a trade union or employees' association.

Prejudice
Disliking people from a particular group or category, based on their race, gender or sexuality etc.

Looking for work

Race and unemployment

■ Looking for a solution

Damian Hannah is 22 years of age.

Damian did well at school, passing eight GCSEs and two A levels. Two years ago he came to England from the West Indies. He hopes to take a degree in computer science, but first needs enough money to pay his way through university.

However, the only jobs that Damian has managed to get so far have been temporary and unskilled. He has stacked shelves in a supermarket, worked in a fast-food restaurant, and helped his aunt with her cleaning job.

'I've been looking for some kind of office work,' said Damian. 'You'd think there would be loads of people who would take me with my qualifications – but they all ask for experience.

'How do I get experience if no one gives me a job? They just won't take a chance, especially if you are black.

'I don't know if it is all because of my colour. You see some black people doing really well, but I think it can make a difference where you live.

'I'm staying with my aunt and her family. It's a nice flat, but this part of London is well known for selling drugs and violent crime. I think employers are put off when they see the postcode on my application form.'

Table 1 Unemployment rates by ethnic origin, age and sex (per cent)

Age group	WOMEN		MEN	
	White	Ethnic minority groups	White	Ethnic minority groups
All	5	12	6	13
16–24 years	10	23	13	26
25–34 years	5	11	6	11
35–59/64 years	3	9	5	11

Source: Labour Force Survey 2001

Table 2 Unemployment rates by ethnic origin, education qualifications and sex (per cent)

Age group	WOMEN		MEN	
	White	Ethnic minority groups	White	Ethnic minority groups
Above A level	2	7	3	6
Up to and including A level	5	14	6	15
No qualifications	8	16	14	21

Source: Labour Force Survey 2001

? questions

1. Look at Table 1, opposite. It is designed to show the percentage of people out of work, according to their age, sex and ethnic group.

   Write down what you notice about the differences in unemployment rates:

   a) between men and women
   b) between white people and people from ethnic minority groups.

2. Now look at Table 2. What do you notice about the unemployment rates among white people and people from ethnic minorities with similar qualifications?

3. Damian says that his colour is one of the reasons why he has been unable to get the kind of work that he is looking for. Do these figures suggest that he is right? Give reasons for your answer.

4. What are the costs of racial discrimination at work – to the employee and the employer?

■ Reducing racial discrimination at work

Here are some things that the Government could do to reduce racial discrimination at work.

Greater penalties Make firms or businesses that racially discriminate pay a much larger amount in compensation.

Training Make employers provide training for their workers so that they understand race issues more clearly.

Financial help Reduce tax rates for those organisations that employ more than an average number of workers from ethnic minorities.

Reflect the community Require companies above a certain size to make sure that the ethnic make-up of their workforce reflects that of the community where they are based.

Records Make all firms and businesses above a certain size keep records of the ethnic origins of their employees, and publish these – rather like school league tables.

RACIST EMPLOYER?
WE'LL HIT YOU WHERE IT HURTS.

PUTTING AN END TO RACISM IN T

RACE ISSUES IN THE WORKPLACE

Training Day on July 26th

LOWER TAX

TAX REDUCTION INCENTIVE FOR ORGANISATIONS TO EMPLOY MORE WORKERS FROM ETHNIC MINORITIES

THE GOVERNMENT yesterday announced that it is considering reducing tax rates for companies that employ more than an average number of workers from ethnic minorities.

In a move to get employers to take on

? questions

5. Write down the advantages and disadvantages of each of the ideas listed above.

6. Are there any that you would reject completely? Explain why. Are there any further ideas you would like to add?

7. If you had to pick just three ideas, which would they be – and why?

Looking for work

Equal opportunities

■ Car crazy

Karen had liked cars for as long as she could remember, and whenever anyone asked her what she wanted to do as a job, she always replied, 'be a mechanic'.

In her final year at school, she saw an advertisement in the paper for two apprentice mechanics at a local garage. The apprenticeship would last five years, at a starting salary of £4,000 a year. Karen thought she stood a reasonable chance of getting the job. She had the required GCSEs in maths and science and had been to the garage earlier in the year on two days' work experience.

When Karen was called for interview, the manager asked her why she wanted the job and if she thought she would fit in. He also asked Karen if she minded getting her hands dirty.

During the interview Karen learnt that she was the best qualified of all the applicants and was told that she stood a good chance of getting one of the jobs.

Two days later, Karen received a letter telling her that her application had been rejected. She later learnt that the apprenticeships had been given to two 16-year-old boys.

Karen suspected that she was a victim of **sex discrimination**. She made some enquiries and decided to take her case to an employment tribunal.

? questions

1. Karen claimed that she had suffered sex discrimination. One test of sex discrimination at a job interview is whether a person is asked questions that would not be asked of someone of the opposite sex. Can you find any examples of this at Karen's interview?

2. On the evidence that you have been given was Karen unlawfully discriminated against?

3. If you decide that Karen did suffer unlawful discrimination how should she be compensated? How would you decide on a fair and reasonable figure?

■ Boys too

Sarat Sharma applied for a job as an office junior with a company making textiles. He had all the right qualifications, including English and maths GCSE.

The letter inviting Sarat for interview began 'Dear Miss Sharma,' and when Sarat rang to confirm that he would attend, the person he spoke to said that they were looking for a young female – and that Sarat would not be suitable.

When Sarat's careers officer learnt about what had happened, he suggested that Sarat report the company for sex discrimination. With the help of the **Equal Opportunities Commission**, Sarat was successful and received £4,000 in compensation. 'I think it is a lot easier for women to get typing and clerical work,' said Sarat.

◾ Stereotypes

Karen and Sarat were looking for jobs that people of their sex do not usually do. In doing so they were breaking the conventional image – or stereotype – that we have of women's and men's work.

Engineering apprenticeships

96% men

4% women

Health and social care apprenticeships

11% men

89% women

Computer analysts

79% men

21% women

Nursery and primary school teachers

14% men

86% women

❓ questions

4. How do you explain why there are so many more men working as computer analysts or engineers, and so many more women in health care and primary schools?

5. Does it matter if most mechanics are men or most nurses are women? What are some of the consequences of these stereotypes?

6. Are there any jobs that women can't do? Are there any jobs that men can't do?

◾ The law

Under the *Sex Discrimination Act 1975* it is against the law for an employer to discriminate against job applicants because of their sex or marital status.

It is also almost always against the law to publish a job advert that discriminates in favour of or against either sex. This means that words like *waitress* or *salesman* cannot normally be used.

However, the law does allow employers to discriminate in favour of women or men for reasons of decency, privacy or authenticity, for example, by choosing a male actor for a male role in a play.

Hi I'm your waitress

❖ keywords

Equal Opportunities Commission
An organisation working to eliminate sex discrimination. It is able to help and advise people who feel they have been unfairly discriminated against because of their sex or marital status.

Sex discrimination
Treating someone less favourably because of their sex.

Looking for work

Train departure

There aren't many women train drivers in Britain – and when Gemma Haxey left London Underground, there was one less.

Gemma quit her job when the train company decided to change drivers' working hours. The new shift patterns required Gemma to work at any time and on any day of the week. This meant that she could no longer be certain of being at home with her nine-year-old daughter in the evening or at weekends.

Gemma felt that this was unfair because it made life particularly difficult for single parents, who did not have a partner to look after their children while they were at work. As most single parents were women, Gemma felt that London Underground's action amounted to sex discrimination. She took her case to an employment tribunal.

The tribunal agreed with Gemma. They said that London Underground's new working arrangements unfairly discriminated against women – because more women than men were single parents.

This is known in law as *indirect* discrimination.

Direct and indirect discrimination

Direct discrimination takes place when someone is treated less favourably because of their sex, race or disability.

The discrimination suffered by Karen and Sarat, outlined on the previous pages, are examples of this.

Indirect discrimination occurs when a situation or condition is imposed that discriminates against a particular sex or race.

In Gemma's case, the tribunal decided that the new work rotas particularly discriminated against women.

? questions

1. Look at the following cases and decide whether they show *direct* or *indirect* sex discrimination.

    Judy started her new job as a training manager. During her second week she arrived at the office in a trouser suit, but was asked to go home and change as the company's dress code did not allow women to wear trousers at work.

    Neil, aged 21, was asked during his interview if he would be prepared to cut off his ponytail if he was given the job. He said that he would not. His interview came to an immediate end.

    Linda, who was in her thirties, with two children, was unable to apply for a job with the local council, because the advertisement indicated that only people aged between 18 and 28 would be considered.

    Nathan wanted to spend as much time as possible with his daughter after she was born and asked the insurance company, where he worked, if he could be employed part-time – as some female employees were, after having a baby. The company refused his request.

    Rhianna became very uncomfortable at work, and eventually decided to leave, after her boss, Daniel, kept putting his arm round her and repeatedly commenting on her figure.

Equal pay

Top of the form Recent studies show that girls generally get better results at school than boys. This pattern continues at college and university, but by the time they get out to full-time work, the position has begun to change.

Closing the gap? In 1971, a year after equal pay laws were introduced, women's average full-time earnings were 69 per cent of those of men.

By 2001, the differences in pay had been reduced – but women's average full-time earnings were still significantly less than those of men.

Who's the boss? Almost certainly it is a man. In 2001, only 18 per cent of managers and directors were women.

Who's the Daddy?

? questions

2. What suggestions can you offer to explain the continuing differences in men's and women's pay?

   Compare your answers with other people in your group, and identify what you think are the most significant reasons.

3. Imagine that we have moved on another 30 years, to the 2030s. Which of the following situations would you most welcome? Explain why.

   • As we were Life has moved back to what it was in the 1930s – when most married women stayed at home looking after the house and family.

   • Women on top The position of men and women have been reversed. Women's wages are now, on average, 20 per cent more than those of men.

   • All on merit At work it makes no difference whether someone is a man or a woman. Their progress depends entirely on their qualifications and how well they do their job.

   • No change The position of men and women is just as they were at the beginning of the twenty-first century. Some women do very well, but the earnings advantage remains with men.

The law

Under the *Equal Pay Act 1970*, women and men working for a company or organisation should receive the same wages and benefits (like holidays or pensions) – provided they are doing either *like work* or *work of equal value*.

Like work refers to work that is broadly similar in nature. For example, technicians who are working for a particular company and doing a similar type of job should receive the same wages and benefits – regardless of sex.

Work of equal value is work that may be different but is of equal skill or difficulty. For example, a court decided that carpenters, painters and cooks who worked for a shipyard all had work of equal value and were entitled to receive the same level of pay and benefits.

Looking for work

Disability and beyond

A problem made worse

Many people suffering from disabilities face an extra difficulty in their lives, which has nothing to do with their condition. It is other people's attitudes.

- Peter books a table for six in a restaurant and adds that one member of the group has a guide dog. The manager tells Peter that the guide dog will have to stay outside, at the back of the restaurant.

- Durrand, a wheelchair user, finds that some taxi drivers refuse to let him ride in their cab, saying that there is no room in the vehicle for his wheelchair.

- Caroline takes her brother, James, to a wine bar. James has learning difficulties and some physical disfigurement. Caroline is told that her brother will put off other customers from using the bar. They are asked not to come back.

Discrimination at work

Under the *Disability Discrimination Act 1995* it is against the law for an employer to treat a person with a disability less favourably than someone else, unless it can be shown that the treatment is justified.

Discrimination against someone who has a disability is allowed if the person is:
- unsuitable for the work involved or
- less suitable than the person who was appointed.

But the law also says that employers have a duty to make any reasonable changes to the working environment that would reduce or remove difficulties preventing a person with a disability from working.

This means that employers could be expected to assist such an employee by:
- providing a special keyboard to help them use a computer
- giving extra training
- rearranging where they might work.

The law applies to all organisations where there are 15 or more employees.

? questions

1. Look at the following cases and decide whether you think the company concerned has broken the law. In each case, give reasons for your answer.

   Will is a wheelchair user and is unable to walk. He applies to work for a small firm of designers employing six people. He is well qualified for the job, but is turned down. It is felt that Will would find it very difficult to get to the firm's office, which is at the top of a spiral staircase with no access by lift.

Melissa is 22 and was born with a condition that prevents her growing to a normal height. She applies for work as a sales assistant in a women's fashion store. She attends an interview, but is not offered the job. Melissa phones the store manager to ask why she was not accepted. The manager tells Melissa that the company requires all employees to be smart and physically attractive. The manager apologises to Melissa and says that, unfortunately, her appearance does not fit the fashionable image of the shop and might discourage some customers from shopping there.

Paul is manager of a supermarket. He has worked for the company for several years and has done very well. A year ago, Paul discovered that he was HIV positive. This means that he has the virus that can go on to develop into AIDS. Although he is able to carry on with his work, he decides to tell his employer. The company worries that store sales will suffer if the public hears of his illness. Paul is dismissed.

David is 20 years old and applies for a job collecting trolleys in a supermarket car park. From David's application form, the store manager sees that David had attended a special school and correctly assumes that David has learning difficulties. David is not called for interview.

2. 'There is not a single job in the country that a person with a disability could not do.' Do you agree with this statement? Explain your point of view.

Too bad

▇ Age discrimination

As they get older, many people face discrimination at work. At the moment this is not against the law, but it will probably change by 2005.

Too old Yvonne West, aged 46, applied for the post of deputy head. Although qualified for the job, she was not interviewed as the headteacher and governors had decided that the job should go to someone under 40.

▇ Other discrimination

Discriminating against someone at work because of their *sexuality* is not unlawful.

Sexuality Paul left his job as a barman after repeated abuse from his colleagues when they learnt that he was gay.

coursework idea

Undertake an investigation into discrimination at work using at least two sources of information. These could be personal accounts, news reports or legal cases. Try to identify the nature of the alleged discrimination, the arguments used by both sides and the outcome of the case. What difficulties did each side face? In your judgement, was the outcome fair?

Working for a living

This unit looks at the legal rights and responsibilities of employers and employees at work.

In work

Anit is 17 and still at school. He is looking for a part-time job. He lives in an area with high unemployment. Finding work is difficult. One evening, while he is in town, Anit sees an advert in the window of a restaurant.

He goes into the restaurant and asks to speak to someone about the job vacancy. Mr Bonner, the owner, explains that he can't speak to Anit right then, but asks him to come tomorrow evening at 6 p.m.

? question

1. Draw up a list of the things you think Anit needs to find out about the job during his interview.

■ Interview

Anit goes back to the restaurant. Mr Bonner asks why he has applied for the job and if he has ever done a similar kind of work.

Anit says that he thinks the work would be interesting, but adds that he has never worked in a restaurant before.

■ Offer

Mr Bonner tells Anit that he would be required to work on Saturdays and Sundays, the busiest days of the week. He would be paid £3.40 an hour and each day would normally work a four-hour shift, either between 11 a.m. and 3 p.m. or 6 p.m and 10 p.m. Anit would also be required to wear a uniform of black trousers, orange shirt and black shoes, which he would have to provide himself.

Anit would be expected to wait on the tables, and help make sure that the restaurant itself was kept clean and tidy.

Anit is offered the job – and accepts.

? question

2. Look back at the list of questions that you thought Anit should ask. How many of these were answered? Is there anything else Anit needs to know before he starts work? If so, what is it?

■ Contract

In agreeing to take the job, Anit formed a contract with Mr Bonner, the owner of the restaurant. A contract of employment is a legal agreement

covering the arrangements for work, such as pay, hours and the nature of the job.

Health and safety

Two days later, Anit begins his first evening at work. Carolyn, who has worked at the restaurant for more than a year, explains to Anit the various hygiene rules that the restaurant has for handling and storing food. Mr Bonner warns Anit that he is likely to lose his job if he breaks any of these rules.

Training

Carolyn shows Anit how to carry several plates of food to a table, how to serve food and also how to keep a record of customer orders. She also explains to Anit what is in some of the dishes – something that customers often ask.

Rights and duties

When a contract for employment is made, certain points are specifically agreed between the employer and employee. In law, these are known as *express terms* – specific things about the job, that both sides have agreed.

However, employers and employees also have other rights and duties that both sides expect will be taken for granted. These are known as the *implied terms* of a contract.

Mr Bonner, for example, must provide Anit with a safe working environment. He must not unlawfully discriminate against him. Anit must obey all reasonable instructions. He also has a duty not to damage Mr Bonner's business. Anit would be breaking the implied terms of his contract (and committing a criminal offence) if he let a friend eat at the restaurant for half price.

Written details

Within two months of starting work, employees should by law be given a written statement of the terms and conditions of their work.

This should include details of:
- their starting date
- rate of pay
- hours of work
- holiday arrangements
- sick pay and pension, and
- the amount of notice that they and their employer must give if the contract is ended.

CONTRACT

? question

3. Why would it be helpful for Anit to have the terms and conditions of his job in the restaurant set down on paper?

A working life

■ **Pay**

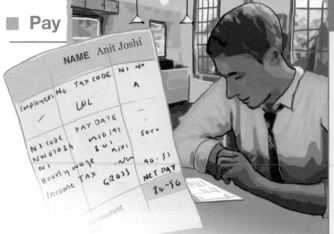

? questions

1. What is Anit's legal position in the following situations?

   Pay At the end of his second week at work, Anit receives his first pay packet. He works out that his hourly rate is less than the national minimum wage.

   Mistake At the end of the evening, the till is down by £15. The loss is traced to one of Anit's tables. It appears that a customer left without paying. Anit is told that the money will be deducted from his earnings over the next two shifts.

2. Why do young workers tend to get paid less than older workers? Is this fair? Is it fair if they are doing the same job?

3. Draw up a list of the consequences of a minimum wage of £5 per hour for all workers – regardless of age.

Almost everyone who is employed is entitled to a pay slip giving details of what they have been paid, and how it has been worked out. The only people to whom this does not apply are those working for the police and those with certain jobs in the fishing industry and merchant navy.

Generally speaking, employers are not allowed to take money from an employee's wage without the employee agreeing to this in writing beforehand. Again, there are a few exceptions. For example, employers can deduct money for tax or national insurance, or take back money from someone who has been overpaid.

Minimum wage In April 1999, a minimum wage came into force throughout the United Kingdom. Since then, it has been raised several times. In October 2002, the Government plans to increase the minimum wage to £3.60 per hour for workers aged 18 to 21 and £4.20 per hour for employees aged 22 and over. There is no minimum wage for young people aged 17 and under.

Benefits, such as free meals, do not count towards the minimum wage. It is a criminal offence for an employer to pay below the national minimum wage.

■ **Health and safety**

Under the *Health and Safety at Work Act 1974*, employers have a legal duty to take care of the safety of their staff.

This means that they must receive the proper training, the equipment that they use must be safe and the people they work with must behave safely and responsibly.

In an organisation with five or more employees, health and safety arrangements must be given to each employee in writing.

Anyone injured at work should immediately report the matter to their supervisor and get legal advice from their trade union or a solicitor.

4. What is Anit's legal position in the following cases?

Fall As Anit collected a customer's order from the kitchen he slipped on some cream that had just been spilt on the floor. His ankle was badly twisted and he missed two days' work.

Abuse Anit receives some racial abuse from three customers, sitting together. Later he tells Mr Bonner, who says that he should just ignore it.

■ Contract

Contracts of employment are very important because they form the agreement upon which many of an employee's rights are based. A contract – whether written down or agreed verbally – sets out the kind of job the employee will do, their hours, pay, holiday arrangements and the kinds of things over which they can be disciplined by their employer.

Part-time workers It is against the law to discriminate against workers employed part-time. This means that part-timers should receive, for example, the same rate of pay as full-time workers. They should have the same training opportunities and have their holiday allowances calculated in the same way as full-time workers.

5. If Mr Bonner did not provide Anit with either a written contract or a note of his terms and conditions at work, what is the basis of Anit's contract?

6. What is Anit's legal position in the following situations?

The wrong shoes Anit leaves his black shoes at a friend's house, and comes to work in trainers. Mr Bonner sends him home. When he returns with the right shoes, Anit is told he must work an extra hour – the amount of time that he lost in collecting the shoes.

No work If the restaurant is quiet Anit is sometimes sent home early. Although he appreciates the time off, it means that on some shifts he gets only two hours' pay.

Jobs At the start of each shift, Anit is often told to mop out the men's toilets. He feels this is unfair. He is employed as a waiter, not a cleaner.

Hours When Anit works in the evening he is expected to stay until the last customer leaves. Sometimes he is unable to get away until after 11 p.m.

Holiday Anit asks if he will be entitled to any holiday later in the year. Mr Bonner explains that he can take a week off but, unlike the other staff, he won't be paid, as he only works part-time.

✳ coursework idea

Carry out a study into young people at work using at least two sources of information. These could be personal accounts, news reports or legal cases. Use these examples to identify one or more issues affecting young people at work. If it is appropriate find out what the law says about the issue that you are describing and give your own assessment, with reasons, of what you think should be a fair and just outcome.

Trade unions

This unit looks at the role of trade unions today.

Working hours

■ Home or away?

Yolanda's dad drives a lorry for a large chemical company. Her mum is a teacher. Her dad is often away from home. Sometimes Yolanda will not see him for two or three days at a time.

Although Yolanda's mum is usually at home for most of the school holidays, they rarely spend much time together in the week. During term time, her mum leaves for work at about 7.30 a.m. and gets home around 6.00 p.m. Most evenings she spends marking or preparing work.

■ More not less

A 2002 survey of 2,200 children, aged 11–18, reported that one in five felt that their parents were too stressed to make time for them and let them talk about their worries. More than half of the boys questioned said that they wished their mum or dad took more interest in their education.

Other research in 2001 found that 61 per cent of working families have parents who are away from home during the early morning, the evening or at weekends. The number of people in this situation has increased with shops, call centres and other businesses operating 24 hours a day.

■ A nation of workers

Workers in Britain work longer hours than those in any other industrial European country. The average working week in Britain is 43.6 hours, compared with 40.3 hours in Europe.

One in ten men work for more than 55 hours a week, and one in 25 for more than 60.

■ Working time

In 1998, the government adopted the *European Working Time Directive*, which sets a maximum working week of 48 hours, including overtime, averaged over 17 weeks. Certain jobs in healthcare, the media and other professions are exempted.

Employees can agree to work longer than this, but employers cannot pressurise them to do so.

An investigation undertaken in 2001 found that almost four million people in Britain work longer than 48 hours a week – the limit set in the *Working Time Directive*.

■ Union challenge

In 1999, Britain's second largest trade union, Amicus, complained to the European Commission that the *Working Time Directive* was not being properly put into practice in Britain.

The union was concerned that there was no requirement in UK law for employers to keep a record of the extra hours that staff worked, nor did employers have responsibility to make sure that staff took their legal entitlement of breaks and holidays.

Amicus chief, Roger Lyons, said 'Such practices drive a coach and horses through the directive.' The union felt that it particularly affected those who are under pressure to volunteer to work longer.

Employers' organisations, however, were generally against a change in the law, saying that people should be allowed to choose for themselves how long they work and that limiting people's hours would reduce industrial productivity.

? questions

1. Is there any evidence, in your experience, that people work too much?

2. What arguments can you put forward in favour of limiting the number of hours that people work? What are the arguments against this? What is your opinion?

■ A changing role

Beginning The first trade unions in Britain developed in the late eighteenth century. They were originally formed by workers to help them negotiate their wages but, as they became larger, they began to represent their members over many other aspects of work.

Union membership in Britain reached its peak in 1920, with 45 per cent of the workforce belonging to a union, but declined in the late 1920s and early 1930s when unemployment became a serious problem. During World War Two industry and unions worked closely together in order to maximise production. Co-operation with government continued after the War and, with strong membership figures once again, unions were able to play a significant role in shaping national policies. Unions have always been strong financial supporters of the Labour Party.

Change In the 1960s and 1970s Britain was increasingly affected by industrial disputes for which, at the time, the unions were held to blame. The new Conservative government in 1979 believed that the influence of the unions should be reduced and, over the next 15 years, introduced new laws designed to weaken their power. These included requiring unions to hold secret ballots before strikes, and making them legally liable for unauthorised strike action.

Now Union membership is once again increasing. The role of unions has changed. Today there is less emphasis on negotiating pay deals and more on helping workers claim their legal rights.

Bill Morris, trade union leader

? questions

3. Look back at the topics covered in this unit and identify those situations where it would have been useful to obtain advice from a trade union. (You may be able to add others to your list.) What would be the advantages of having support from a union? Are there any disadvantages?

4. Employers also belong to associations, such as the Confederation of British Industry. What is the value of such organisations to them?

Losing your job

This unit looks at the law surrounding dismissal from work.

Fired!

Graham worked as a van driver for a large firm of printers. He had done the job for three years, but on several occasions his boss had been unhappy with his work, complaining that he was too slow.

One morning, Graham got completely lost on a delivery and was, once again, running late. In trying to make up time he was caught speeding by a roadside camera.

When the company was served with a speeding penalty, details were checked and it became clear that Graham had driven the van in question. The following morning he was called into the manager's office and told that he needed to find another job. He was given three weeks' notice to leave.

*I DON'T **BELIEVE** IT! I'M LOST AND I'M LATE! **WHAT CAN I DO?***

*I'M NOT INTERESTED IN EXCUSES! **YOU'RE FIRED!***

■ Notice

Finishing work When someone wants to leave their job, they must normally inform their employer, in advance, of their intention to leave. This is called a period of notice. The amount of notice an employee must give is normally set out in their terms and conditions of work.

If there is no written statement, a person who has worked for an employer for four weeks or more is required to give seven days' notice, irrespective of length of service.

Sacked An employee's terms and conditions of work will usually give the length of notice to which they are entitled.

If there is no written statement, the law states that the minimum period of notice employers must give is as follows:

- after four weeks' continuous service, one week
- after two years' continuous service, one week for every year of service
- after twelve years' of continuous service, twelve weeks. This is the maximum entitlement.

An employer who does not give proper notice may be taken to a county court by the employee and sued for wrongful dismissal. If the employee is successful, they will be awarded damages for the amount of money they have lost by not being given the right notice.

1. Dorothy was sacked from her office job after three months, because of the poor standard of her work. She was very slow and made many mistakes. She had no written statement of terms and conditions of work. How much notice was Dorothy entitled to?

2. Kassie worked for five years part-time, as a doctor's receptionist. After several warnings she was sacked for poor time keeping. She had no written statement of terms and conditions of work. How much notice was she entitled to?

3. Bruno lost his job as a chef after he arrived at work drunk for the third time. Why do you think his boss gave him two weeks' wages and told him to leave immediately – instead of allowing him to work during his two weeks' notice?

Instant dismissal

If an employee does something seriously wrong at work, their employer may decide to bring their contract to an end immediately and to sack them on the spot.

Instant dismissal means that the employee loses their right to notice – but they should have first had an opportunity to defend themselves against the allegation before the dismissal takes place.

Serious misbehaviour is described in the law as *gross misconduct* and includes theft, violence, dishonesty and damage to the employer's property.

Go!

Claire worked as an office manager for an insurance company and was instantly dismissed after her boss discovered that she had been arranging her holiday during working hours. Over a period of several days, Claire had been surfing the Internet looking for cheap flights and hotels.

Claire said that she had only been doing this during her lunch breaks. She claimed to have spent less than two hours over the four days searching for a holiday, adding that there was no time to go to a travel agent after she had finished work.

Her boss reminded Claire that the company had written to all employees saying that office computers could not be used for personal use as they contained important and confidential data. Claire was told to leave immediately. Claire felt that her dismissal was unfair and took her claim to an employment tribunal.

? question

4. Did Claire's behaviour amount to gross misconduct? Give reasons for your answer.

Losing your job

Claiming unfair dismissal

■ Fair or unfair?

In this section, you will be asked to decide whether you think people have been dismissed from their job fairly or unfairly. But before you do that, you might like to consider (without looking at the section on the law on the next page) what makes a dismissal fair or unfair.

One way of doing this is to complete the following sentences:

A person is dismissed fairly when………
A person is dismissed unfairly when……

■ Greater rights

Until 1971, employers were able to dismiss staff as they pleased. They were required only to give the correct notice, and pay the employee the money due to them.

More than 30 years on, employees now have much more protection against unfair dismissal. A simplified summary of the law is given on page 55.

❓ question

1. Using the information on this double page, decide whether you feel the person in each case was fairly or unfairly dismissed, giving reasons for each of your decisions.

Colette had been employed as a secretary for two months when she was given the sack after taking a two-hour lunch break. Her employer felt that she worked too slowly and had previously warned her about poor time keeping.

Martine lost her job in a bank, where she had worked for two years, when her boss discovered that she had lied at her interview when asked if she had any criminal convictions. A year before joining the company she had been found guilty of theft.

John had worked for the ambulance service for ten years. He lost his job after he injured his back lifting a heavy patient. He was dismissed when it became clear that he could no longer do the same kind of work.

Evan was fired after failing to turn up for his job as a bus driver when his partner Nerys went into hospital to have a baby. In the ten months that he had been with the firm he had missed work twice due to the difficulties that Nerys was having with her pregnancy.

■ The law

Anyone who feels they have been unfairly dismissed, and has been working for their employer for a year, may try to obtain compensation for this by taking their case to an employment tribunal. The tribunal can order that the employee should be given their old job back – but this is rarely done.

An employer must show that they had a fair reason for sacking the employee and that – in the circumstances – they behaved in a reasonable way.

Fair Under the *Employment Rights Act 1996*, fair reasons for dismissal are as follows:

- employee misconduct – such as theft, fighting or persistent lateness

Dean had worked for three years in a sports shop. One morning he was told that he would be losing his job because profits were down. A week after he had left, Dean noticed that someone else had been employed in his place.

Natasha made several mistakes during her first week as a cashier at a supermarket. Just before she went home on Saturday she was told that she was unsuitable, and was dismissed.

- incapability – the employee does not, or is not able to, do the job to the required standard
- redundancy – when the job done by the employee is no longer required
- so as not to break the law – when, for example, a van driver loses their licence for a drink-driving offence
- any other good reason.

Unfair Some reasons for dismissal are seen in law as *automatically* unfair, and here an employer has no defence. In these cases, employees may claim unfair dismissal, even if they have been working for their employer for less than a year.

Some of the situations in which dismissal is automatically unfair are set out below.

- *Trade union* – it is automatically unfair to dismiss someone because they belong (or choose not to belong) to a trade union. It is also unfair to dismiss them because of their trade union activities outside working hours.
- *Pregnancy* – dismissing someone solely because they are pregnant, need to attend maternity classes or plan to take maternity leave is automatically unfair.
- *Health and safety* – anyone who is sacked because of reasonable concern about health and safety at work is automatically unfairly dismissed.
- *Family emergencies* – a person has the right to take a 'reasonable amount' of time off to deal with the illness of their child or other family member.

Warnings A worker who under-performs or breaks a rule in a minor way and is sacked, without a warning or a reasonable time to improve, will almost certainly have a case for unfair dismissal – although there is no law saying that warnings *must* be given before a person is dismissed.

An employer may dismiss someone immediately for gross misconduct. No warning is necessary.

Losing your job

The employment tribunal

■ Reason to leave?

One morning, Kirsty Brennan received a call at work from her son's school. Seven-year-old Robbie had a high temperature and an ear infection. The school felt he ought to see a doctor.

Kirsty immediately went to her boss, telling him that her son was unwell and that she needed to collect him from school.

Just as she was preparing to leave, a colleague came downstairs to tell Kirsty that she had been sacked. 'Mr Collier has given you one week's notice,' she said, 'because he can't rely on you.'

Kirsty felt that she had been sacked unfairly. She decided to take her case to an employment tribunal.

At the tribunal Mr Collier said that Kirsty was rude and aggressive. 'This really was the last straw,' he said. 'She would fling files onto my desk, and if I asked her to make any changes, she would snatch the paper and storm out.'

'Ms Brennan did not *ask* if she could pick up her son,' Simon Collier went on, 'she just *told* me she was leaving. She had only been here six weeks, and this was the second occasion she needed time off for childcare arrangements.'

Kirsty said that she didn't have the chance to tell Mr Collier that she would return as soon as she had taken her son to the doctor and found someone to look after him.

■ A court of law

A person who feels that they have been unfairly dismissed may take their case to an employment tribunal. This is a special court dealing with employment disputes.

■ Procedure

Anyone claiming unfair dismissal must fill in a special form, available from a Jobcentre, on which they set out details of their case.

It is important to get help with this from someone with experience in dealing with these cases. This could be a solicitor, someone from the Citizens Advice Bureau or a trade union representative.

■ Paperwork

A lot of preparation is required in gathering evidence and arranging for witnesses to come to court. Often both sides are required to let each other inspect the documents that they will use as evidence.

? question

1. Using the information in this section on *Losing your job* put yourself in the position of a member of an employment tribunal, and decide whether Kirsty Brennan was unfairly dismissed. When you have reached your decision, write a short report outlining the reasons for your view.

Finding a solution

Before the case goes to tribunal one more attempt is made to help both sides reach agreement, and avoid going to court. Often this is successful.

At the tribunal

Tribunals are more informal than other courts of law. No one wears a gown or a wig, as they do in a county court.

The panel that will hear the case consists of three people: a legally qualified chairperson, and two lay people – one representing employers and the other trade unions. The three members of the panel should not all be of the same sex.

It was originally intended that people should put their case to the tribunal in person. This is still possible but today, many applicants use the services of a lawyer or a trade union official. Employers also often engage specialists.

The decision

If members of the tribunal find in favour of the employee, they usually order that the person should be compensated for loss of income and the difficulties they have faced as a result of the unfair treatment.

Tribunals are allowed to order that the employee should be given their job back – but rarely do.

The cost

Tribunals were designed to be a cheap and simple way of settling disputes. Today the average case costs around £2,000 in fees and time – but this doesn't include the damage to staff relations and the cost of finding another worker.

If the employee wins, he or she is often worse off. The average award is under £3,000. More than half the people who take their case to tribunal are in a lower paid job afterwards.

? question

2. It is estimated that about one and a half million people a year have a serious problem at work. Of the half who seek advice, only a quarter decide to take the matter further. Why do you think many people do not assert their legal rights and make claims for unfair dismissal or discrimination? Does it matter?

✳ coursework idea

Find an employment tribunal case that is reported in two newspapers. How do the reports compare? What is the style of reporting used? Are the facts the same in each report? Explain in your own words the nature of the case, the law upon which it was based and the outcome.

Unequal Britain

This unit looks at some of the inequalities that exist in Britain today and efforts that are being made to bring them to an end.

Racism

■ Death in custody

At the beginning of 2000, Zahid Mubarek, aged 19, from London, was sentenced to 90 days in a **Young Offenders Institution.** He had been found guilty of interfering with a car and taking razor blades valued at £6.

Towards the end of his sentence he was placed in a cell with Robert Stewart, aged 20, who was known by the prison authorities to be dangerous and disturbed. Robert Stewart was being held, charged with sending racist hate mail. The prison authorities knew about his racist feelings. He had a Ku Klux Klan sign on display in his cell and his letters home had referred to the number of 'niggers on the wing'.

On the day before he was due to be released, Zahid Mubarek was battered to death in his cell by Robert Stewart, using the leg of a table.

After his son's death, Mr Mubarek said, 'There was always a lot of racist abuse going on, a lot of trouble. The wardens just used to keep their heads down and let prisoners get on with what they were doing.'

Racial equality is an important issue, for both staff and prisoners

After the murder, a separate investigation was undertaken into the running of the Young Offenders Institution where Zahid Mubarek died. It found that the behaviour of a small number of prison officers was openly racist. It reported that prisoners of Asian or African-Caribbean background were twice as likely to be separated from other prisoners and twice as likely to have restraint used against them.

Findings of this kind have not been unusual in British prisons. Another investigation, also made in 2000, reported that 49 per cent of the Asian prisoners questioned said that they had been racially abused in prison and 12 per cent stated they had been attacked.

It is not only black inmates who have been affected by racism. Black officers also receive racist comments and jokes, which many feel they have to accept in order to fit in at work.

■ Institutionalised racism

Institutionalised racism takes place when an organisation collectively fails to provide a proper service to people because of their colour, culture or ethnic origin. It can be shown through prejudice, ignorance and racist stereotyping.

The prison service is far from being the only organisation criticised for this.

> ### ? questions
>
> 1. Who do you think was responsible for the death of Zahid Mubarek? Who was at fault? Give reasons for your answer.
>
> 2. How could Zahid Mubarek's death have been avoided?

■ Racism in prison

Robert Stewart was convicted of murder and jailed for life.

COMMISSION FOR RACIAL EQUALITY

Second class citizen When Farouk Stemmet climbed on board the 16.22 train from Liverpool to Sunderland he headed for the first-class accommodation. As he approached the carriage he was stopped by the train conductor and told that he should sit elsewhere. Mr Stemmet explained that he had a first-class ticket.

When the conductor came round to check his ticket, Mr Stemmet protested about his treatment. The conductor replied that he was only doing his job, and suggested that Mr Stemmet had a chip on his shoulder because he was black.

Mr Stemmet decided to make a complaint. He wrote to the rail company and reported the matter to the **Commission for Racial Equality** (CRE). The CRE helped Mr Stemmet bring a case against the train company. Mr Stemmet successfully showed that he had been unfairly discriminated against.

? questions

3. How might you account for the behaviour of the conductor?

4. Was his behaviour unusual, in your opinion?

5. How do you think Mr Stemmet should be compensated for his unfair treatment?

6. What action could be taken to try to make sure that the conductor or other employees do not behave in the same way again?

7. How might a school promote good race relations?

■ The law

Under the *Race Relations Act 1976* it is unlawful to discriminate against anyone on grounds of race, colour, nationality, or ethnic or national origin. It is also against the law for public bodies – such as the police, schools, hospitals, prisons – to discriminate while carrying out any of their functions.

Public bodies also have a legal duty to promote good race relations in the way that they operate.

❖ keywords

Commission for Racial Equality
An official body set up under the *Race Relations Act 1976* to work towards ending race discrimination. It can give advice and help people who believe they have suffered race discrimination. It also has the power to require organisations to take action to prevent further race discrimination.

Young Offenders Institution
Secure accommodation where young offenders between the ages 15 and 21 are held in custody.

Unequal Britain

Separate or together?

After the riots in 2001. Oldham and Burnley (below).

■ Trouble on the streets

Between April and June 2001 several towns in the north of England suffered from the worst street rioting seen in England for 20 years. Much of the trouble appeared to be between groups of white and Asian young people in areas where unemployment is high and housing is poor.

One of the places involved was Oldham, in Lancashire, where around 11 per cent of the population is British Asian. Historically, many workers came from overseas to work in the textile industries that have now closed down, leaving a large number of people without work.

Most people of Asian background in Oldham live close together in the poorest areas and are more likely to be unemployed than their white counterparts. Over the years, districts of the town have divided along racial lines and schools have become largely white or Asian. In a report on the riots, Oldham Council was criticised for not doing enough to prevent this 'segregation', or separate development.

■ Parallel lives

In circumstances like these, where there is lack of understanding and positive contact, suspicion and even fear between groups can begin to develop.

In Burnley, another Lancashire town, fights took place between Asian and white drug gangs – with damage to property and cars. Rumours of more trouble were spread by white racist groups. A group of white people attacked an Asian taxi driver with a hammer. Asian men then threw bricks through the window of a pub, because they believed that inside were people who were planning an attack on them. The next day, white people attacked a number of Asian businesses.

As in Oldham, it was found that there were too few opportunities for people of different religions and customs to meet and mix together. White and Asian firms only employed members of their own communities and, again, the schools had become largely segregated.

? questions

1. What are the effects of this kind of segregation? List as many as you can.

2. What might be the causes?

3. Should anything be done about this separate development? If so what, and who should take responsibility? (Individuals, councils or the government?)

■ Peacemaking

The official report into the riots suggested that many things needed to be done to prevent further trouble.

Suggestions included:

- *Housing* Make housing estates racially mixed – even if people did not at first want this.

- *Jobs* Improve job opportunities. If more wealth could be brought into the towns, people would be less likely to listen to the arguments of racists.

- *Schools* Alter catchment areas to make schools more racially mixed. Also discourage schools from having children of just one religious faith.

- *Councils* The number of council workers from ethnic minorities should be increased significantly. In Oldham 2.5 per cent of the council workforce was from the ethnic minorities.

- *Democracy* The council should listen more to what local people say, and people from all communities should become more involved in local politics.

？ questions

4. Think about these proposals. If you were on the council, which would you do first and why? Are there any that you would not recommend? Explain why.

5. Which would be the most difficult to put into effect, in your opinion?

6. Some of these proposals will restrict people's freedom of choice about where to live or the kind of schooling to choose. Is this acceptable?

■ A sense of belonging

During the discussions that took place after the riots, Home Secretary, David Blunkett, added his own suggestions. He felt there was a problem in that some newcomers to Britain could not speak English (although the young people rioting on the streets could speak English perfectly). Mr Blunkett said that this made it difficult for people from different backgrounds to mix and to play a full part in the community and added that learning English did not mean that anyone had to give up their own culture, values or lifestyles.

？ questions

7. How far do you agree with David Blunkett's view?

8. How important is it to have a strong sense of identity? Where does this come from and how does it show itself?

9. Is it possible to feel you belong to more than one community?

10. Who has responsibility for creating a 'sense of belonging'?

Unequal Britain

Sexual equality

Aiming high

Rosie is 15 and has everything to live for. She is clever, with lots of friends and a cheerful personality that everyone seems to like. Her hobbies are gymnastics and football and she is very good at both.

One day she hopes to represent her country at one of these sports. Her mum is a nurse and her dad works for a pipeline company. Rosie would like to be a lawyer – and perhaps eventually a judge. She'd also like to do something that helps people – which is why she thinks that she could, one day, become an MP.

All the statistics opposite obtained from the Equal Opportunities Commission

? questions

1. How likely is Rosie to realise all her ambitions?

2. Which do you think she will find most difficult to achieve? The information on the right might help you with this.

Life chances

Education Qualifications play a large part in determining the kind of job a person will do. People with low qualifications are more likely to be unemployed or in low-paid work.

Men, as a whole, have better job qualifications than women. However, the picture changes among young women and men under 25 years of age.

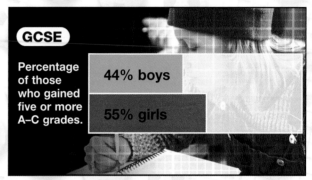

GCSE

Percentage of those who gained five or more A–C grades.

44% boys

55% girls

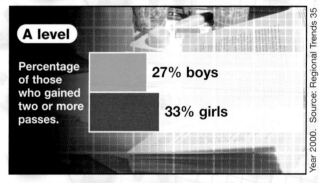

A level

Percentage of those who gained two or more passes.

27% boys

33% girls

Year 2000. Source: Regional Trends 35

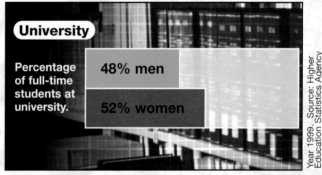

University

Percentage of full-time students at university.

48% men

52% women

Year 1999. Source: Higher Education Statistics Agency

* fact

It was not until 1895 that women were eligible to obtain a degree at most British universities. Women wanting to graduate from Oxford had to wait until 1920, and at Cambridge until 1948.

Employment by occupation 2000

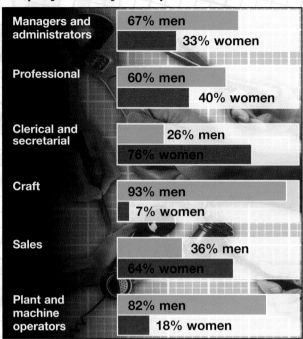

Managers and administrators	67% men
	33% women
Professional	60% men
	40% women
Clerical and secretarial	26% men
	76% women
Craft	93% men
	7% women
Sales	36% men
	64% women
Plant and machine operators	82% men
	18% women

Source: Office for National Statistics

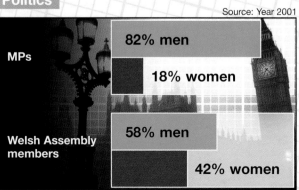

The hourly earnings of women working full-time are, on average, 82 per cent of men's hourly earnings. *(Office for National Statistics 2000)*

Politics

Source: Year 2001

MPs	82% men
	18% women
Welsh Assembly members	58% men
	42% women

? questions

3. Who or what is standing in the way of Rosie's success?

4. What would you say to someone who believes that full equality between men and women cannot be achieved because men and women are different?

5. Now that girls appear to be doing better at school than boys, should special efforts be made to help boys? If so, what should they be?

■ The Law

Under the *Sex Discrimination Act 1975* it is against the law to treat a person less favourably because of their sex. This applies in particular to work, training, education and the provision of goods and services.

The *Equal Pay Act 1970* gives women and men rights to equal pay and benefits for the same or similar work.

Women should not lose their job because of pregnancy, childbirth or the care of their children. The law also states that parents of children born after 14 December 1999 have the right to take up to 13 weeks' unpaid leave during the first five years of their child's life.

Unequal Britain
The long struggle

■ Men's property

Before the *Married Women's Property Act 1882*, married women were not allowed to own property. Once they got married, everything they possessed belonged to their husband.

In the nineteenth century it was almost impossible for a woman to end her marriage by divorce. At a cost of £700–£800 (a huge amount of money at the time) only the gentry or very rich *men* could afford a divorce. It wasn't until 1923 that women as well as men could obtain a divorce on grounds of adultery.

With very little support for single parent families, many women who were trapped in an unhappy marriage had no choice but to endure it. They remained, in effect, their husband's property.

■ Campaigners

However, a few women were not content. They realised that progress would be slow if all the laws continued to be made by men. By 1885, all men (and not just the rich landowners) had been given the right vote – but women had not. No woman had the right to choose her MP, and certainly no woman could stand for election as a Member of Parliament.

For this reason, in the early 1900s, women began to campaign seriously for the vote. They were called 'suffragettes', from the word 'suffrage' meaning 'the right to vote'.

By 1906, their leader, Emmeline Pankhurst, decided that more pressure was required, which marked the beginning of the suffragettes' militant campaign. They broke windows, damaged government buildings, burnt railway stations and even attacked MPs.

■ War intervenes

When the First World War broke out in 1914, the suffragettes halted their campaign and persuaded women instead to work for the war effort, by going into industry or joining the armed services.

With so many men fighting overseas, women did much of the work previously carried out by men, in factories and elsewhere. This changed many people's views about the capability of women.

In 1918, immediately after the war, women over 30 were given the vote, and in 1928 this was extended to women over 21. At last women were on equal terms with men.

However, some men who had wanted to stand for election that year felt this was unfair on them as individuals. So they took the matter to court. The court ruled that this kind of 'positive discrimination' (action taken to address the unfair position of a whole group) was actually against the law and unfairly discriminated against men.

■ Women in Parliament

Women were first allowed to stand for Parliament in 1918. There were 17 female candidates, but only one was successful. Until 1987, the maximum number of women elected at any general election was 30.

After the 1997 election, women comprised 121 out of the 659 MPs. At the 2001 election the figure fell to 118.

Britain now ranks thirty-third in the world in terms of women MPs.

? questions

1. Do you think it matters that women make up more than half the population of the UK, but have only 18 per cent of the MPs? Explain why.

2. Do you think Parliament would be very different if it had equal numbers of men and women? If so, how?

■ Positive discrimination

Before the 1997 election, the Labour Party decided that the time had come to tackle the problem of too few women in Parliament. They decided that some of the 'safe seats' (these are seats that the party is sure it will win) would have to select a woman candidate. They did this by having only women on the list of candidates to be interviewed.

■ In favour and against

Here are two statements about positive discrimination – both made by women MPs, and both from the Conservative Party.

'We whinge and whine and demand special treatment. If that isn't an insult to women, I don't know what is.'
Ann Widdecombe MP

'There are many women not being selected who would make first-class MPs and Parliament is missing out on a pool of talent that would strengthen this house.'
Theresa May MP

? question

3. Do you believe 'positive discrimination' of the kind described above is fair? What are the arguments on both sides of this issue? What other social groups could this apply to?

Unequal Britain
Challenging disability

■ Dining out

Robert was looking forward to an end–of–year celebration with some friends. A table for seven was booked at a local restaurant.

Everything was fine until the friend who had made the booking rang the restaurant to confirm the reservation. He mentioned that there would be one wheelchair user in the party – this was Robert. Suddenly the owner changed his tune completely. He was sorry but the restaurant could not cater for wheelchair users because it would be very crowded. The friend was very indignant and cancelled the booking rather than leave Robert behind.

Later Robert himself phoned to make a booking but the same thing happened.

On learning that Robert had a disability, the restaurant owner refused to accept the booking.

? questions

1. Was it reasonable of the restaurant owner to refuse Robert a meal at busy times? Explain your view.

2. Was it reasonable of Robert to expect the restaurant owner to make allowances for someone with a disability? Again, explain your view.

■ What is a disability?

When we hear the word 'disabled' we often think first of wheelchair users. But disability also includes blindness, deafness and having learning difficulties. Many other people are affected by mental illness or have brain damage from accidents or strokes that make it difficult for them to function properly. In fact there are 8.5 million people with some form of disability in Britain. That is about one person in seven.

■ Dependent on charity

In Victorian England, a disabled child could be a great burden, especially for poor families. Many had to beg or steal for a living.

One man, John Groom, was aware that girls with disabilities were especially at risk. He felt a duty to do something about this. He had the idea that the girls could be offered work making artificial flowers that could be sold on the streets and in shops. The income from the flowers, along with charitable donations, would help pay for the girls to lives in decent homes, looked after by specially trained nurses and housekeepers.

In 1866 John Groom founded his charity to care for disabled young women. Today, this and many other charities provide help and support for people with disabilities.

 Disability Rights Commission

Rights not charity

People doing charitable work have played a very important role in shaping modern society. They have campaigned for a better deal for all kinds of people. But charity cannot be demanded as if it is a right. All charities are limited in the number of people they can help.

For a long time people with disabilities, like Robert, were unable to do anything about the discrimination that they faced. In some ways they were a forgotten group. This is why a new law was needed.

Disability Discrimination Act 1995

Under this Act, it became unlawful to treat someone less favourably because of a disability. This applies to the provision of services as well as to employment.

Robert took his case to the Disability Rights Commission. This is the body that advises people of their rights under the Act and helps them with legal cases. As the result of legal action, the restaurant owner apologised to Robert, and agreed to pay him £200 in compensation. The restaurant owner also took advice from the Disability Rights Commission on how he and his staff should treat customers with disabilities.

 questions

3. Was this a fair settlement of Robert's complaint in your opinion?

4. Why do you think it has taken so much longer to outlaw discrimination against people with disabilities, than race or sex discrimination?

Education

In 2001, the *Special Educational Needs and Disability Act* made it unlawful to discriminate in the education of people with disabilities. Schools have a duty not to treat a student less favourably because of their disability and should make reasonable adjustments. This might mean, for example, changing the timetable so that all the rooms where lessons are taught are accessible to the disabled student. There is no duty on schools, however, to alter the physical structure of buildings.

 **question**

5. What kind of changes might schools need to make to ensure that pupils with disabilities have an equal education?

coursework idea

Carry out a small investigation either at school or where you work, if you have a part-time job, into the provisions and adjustments that are made for people with a disability. What do the people who run these organisations know about this aspect of the law? What changes have been made? If it is possible, try to speak to someone with a disability about the problems that they face and what could be done to lessen some of these.

Older people

This unit examines the lives of older people in the UK and, in particular, how they are seen and treated by others.

The future is grey

■ Getting older

? questions

1. Which of these people would you describe as old? Would it be all of them, or just one or two? What makes people describe someone as being old?

2. What kinds of things do you associate with becoming old? What kinds of things *don't* you associate with older people?

3. What sort of stereotypes do we have about older people? How accurate are they?

4. What do you imagine are the best and worst things about getting old?

■ Too old?

By the end of the Second World War, in 1945, Sir Winston Churchill was 71 years of age. For most of the past six years, as Prime Minister, he had led Britain through one of its most difficult periods in history.

Although defeated in the 1945 election, he returned as Prime Minister in 1951, and finally retired in 1955 at the age of 81.

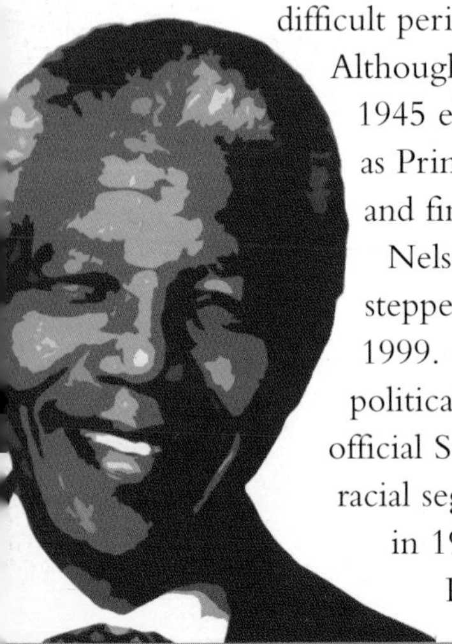

Nelson Mandela was also 81 when he stepped down as President of South Africa in 1999. In 1965 he had been imprisoned for his political activities against apartheid – the then official South African government policy of racial segregation. In 1990 he was released, and in 1994, at the age of 76, was elected President.

? question

5. Few achieve as much as Nelson Mandela or Winston Churchill, but most older people have worked, had a family, and faced some difficult times during their lives. What do you think older people have to offer to society?

■ One hundred and rising

In 1950, there were 300 people in Britain aged 100 or over. Today there are more than 6,000 centenarians. It is predicted that by the year 2036 this figure will have risen to nearly 40,000 and, by 2066, to 95,000.

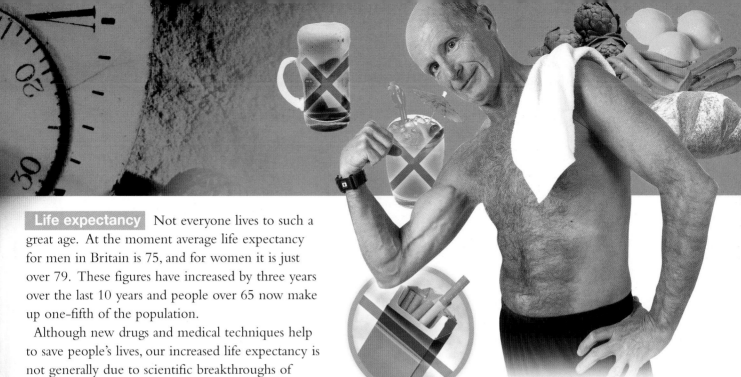

Life expectancy Not everyone lives to such a great age. At the moment average life expectancy for men in Britain is 75, and for women it is just over 79. These figures have increased by three years over the last 10 years and people over 65 now make up one-fifth of the population.

Although new drugs and medical techniques help to save people's lives, our increased life expectancy is not generally due to scientific breakthroughs of these kinds. Researchers into ageing say we are not really living longer, but rather achieving our full lifespan – because we are avoiding the things that used to kill us in the past. A reduction in smoking, better living conditions and a healthier diet have all helped to extend people's lives.

Health Although people are living longer, statistics show that the proportion of our life during which we may be in poor health has increased. Two-thirds of people over 75 have a long-standing illness.

■ Change

Many countries around the world now face decisions about how to adapt to having larger numbers of older people.

Here are some of the things that people say need to be done in Britain.

- *Accommodation* Older people usually need help with their living arrangements, either to stay in their own home or with special purpose-built accommodation.

- *Education and leisure* Many people now live for 20 or 30 years after they retire. If this time is to be enjoyable, more education and leisure facilities are required.

- *Help and support* It is now much less common for older people to live either with or close by their family. More need support and care with everyday living.

- *Healthcare* More medical facilities are required as the proportion of older people in society increases.

- *Pensions* People now draw a pension from the state for much longer than they have in the past. More money needs to be set aside for this – which means that taxes will have to be raised and people will have to save more themselves.

- *Retirement* Most people now retire before they are 65. If people stayed at work longer less money would be needed for pensions, and more would be paid in tax - which could be used for public services like education, hospitals, and transport.

- *Transport* Better public transport services will be be needed, as most elderly people don't have the use of a car. Without frequent and low cost public transport, many elderly people will be almost housebound.

HIS *DAD'S* POPPING ROUND TO VISIT LATER ON...

? questions

6. How much responsibility does the state have to help older people, and how much should they be responsible for themselves?

7. If the Government had the resources to adopt only three of the above measures, which would you recommend, and why?

Older people

An age-old problem

Wards A–C
X-ray Dept

■ Standards of care

It was a cold day in February. Two elderly patients, Edith Vance and Dorothy Gately, needed to have an X-ray. The hospital was on a large site and the distance from the ward to the X-ray department was so great that an ambulance was used to carry patients between buildings.

As they were helped into their wheelchairs, neither patient was wearing a dressing gown or slippers. The blanket that they were each given did not properly cover their legs and feet.

A porter took the two patients together from the ward. He pushed Edith ahead of him. Dorothy was towed behind, travelling backwards.

When they reached the waiting ambulance, Edith was left in the roadway, while Dorothy was put onto the ambulance lift. This process was reversed as they were taken from the ambulance outside the X-ray department.

While she waited, Edith asked what was happening. Neither the porter nor ambulance driver replied.

The porter wheeled both patients into the X-ray building, and used the footrest of the first wheelchair to push open the door. As they moved through the entrance the heavy plastic doors swung back hitting Edith, who was coming through in reverse, on the back of her head.

While they waited for their X-ray, neither Dorothy nor Edith was told how long they would have to wait.

? questions

1. Read the account of the two elderly patients. Make a note of anything about their treatment that you feel was wrong. Explain why.

2. A friend of one of the patients reported the matter to the hospital. An investigation took place. All the facts in the account were found to be correct. What action do you think the hospital should take?

■ Rationing

Medical treatment can be very expensive. There is no health service in the world that can give every patient everything that they need. There are always a lot of people who are ill and only a limited number of medical staff, drugs and medical equipment available to treat them.

Hospital staff therefore have to make decisions about who will receive the limited treatment that is available. Sometimes they decide that this will be based on age.

Unfair? Charlie Hughes is 85 years old. He has a heart problem, which his GP said could be helped by having by-pass surgery. This is an operation to repair an artery to the heart. Mr Hughes's GP sent him to see a specialist.

At the hospital, the surgeon said that he couldn't understand why Mr Hughes was there. 'There are men in their fifties still capable of earning a living who need this operation,' he said, adding that, at his age, Mr Hughes had little chance of ever having the operation.

Mr Hughes said he realised that only a limited number of people could be treated at any one time. But he felt that it would be much fairer if everyone, no matter what their age, put their name on a waiting list and received their treatment in turn.

? questions

3. Do you agree with Charlie Hughes? Should older people have the same right to medical treatment as younger people?

4. Does a 17-year-old who needs treatment for cancer deserve to be treated ahead of someone who is 70? Try to explain the thinking behind your answer.

■ Discrimination at work

The United States has a law that forbids discrimination at work, on grounds of age, against anyone over 40. For example, if two people aged 30 and 45 apply for a job, selecting the 30-year-old on grounds of age alone would be against the law.

In Britain we have a Code of Conduct for employers that *recommends* that employers should have a workforce covering a wide age range and should avoid setting a limit to the age of job applicants.

The European Union has proposed that steps should be taken to reduce age discrimination, but none of these, as yet, has the force of law.

? question

5. We have laws making it illegal to discriminate on grounds of sex, race and disability. Should we add age to this list? Make a list of the arguments both for and against this idea. What would your own recommendation be? If you are in favour of such a law, how far would it extend? What would it cover?

GREAT *CV*, FANTASTIC EXPERIENCE, GOOD *REFERENCES...*

TROUBLE IS... YOU'RE WAY TOO *OLD!*

Older people

Older but still active

■ Respect

In some communities, older people are treated with great respect. Their age has given them an experience and understanding that is valued in the community – and there are still a small number of traditional societies where older people automatically play an important part in reaching decisions about matters affecting the whole community.

In the UK, however, it is often said that older people are not given the respect that they had in the past.

While it is true that age probably did once give people an authority that they don't have today, it does not mean that older people were always well looked after. In Victorian times, for example, many ended their lives in the workhouse, where they did unpaid work in return for food and accommodation.

? questions

1. In your experience, how much respect is given to older people in our society today? Try to give evidence to support your view.

2. How do people show respect for the elderly? How do they show a lack of respect?

■ Fund of knowledge

A person aged 70 or 80 today may well have a memory that goes back more than a hundred years. They will remember some of the experiences of their mother or father, who will have been born at the turn of the twentieth century, and may have memories of their grandparents too. They will remember the first TV broadcast, the Second World War, the dropping of the first atomic bomb, and many other events that have shaped our history.

If they were born in another part of the world they would have memories not only of another time, but of another culture as well.

? questions

3. What kind of knowledge and understanding do older people have? How is it different from those who are very much younger?

4. Can younger people learn anything from older people? If so, what do you think it is?

■ Living in the now

Many older people manage to live life to the full even though their bodies may be slowing down. When they retire they take the opportunity to do something new, including working as volunteers. John Malyon, 68, says: 'I am an accountant by training. I didn't want to stop working suddenly, so I contacted a charity and the local football club to ask if they could use anyone like me. For ten years I have helped them both keep their financial records in order.'

Pensioners' union

We often hear of people doing things *for* older people. But in 1979 they formed a union to fight their own battles. The National Pensioners' Convention is a pressure group run by pensioners for pensioners. Among other things, it organises meetings, rallies and demonstrations, gives advice and **lobbies** politicians.

? questions

5. What kind of voluntary work do older people become involved with in your community?

6. What would you imagine are the benefits to a) themselves and b) the people who they help?

7. Are there any ways you can think of in which older people could get involved as volunteers in your school or your own community?

? questions

11. What do you think should be top of the list of things the National Pensioners' Convention should be campaigning for?

■ Campaigning

The Beth Johnson Foundation in Stoke-on-Trent is a charity that aims to improve the quality of life for older people. One of their recent projects involved getting together with young people to campaign on issues that affect them both, such as burglary and the high cost of transport. All the project members came to understand each other better and, in many cases, became good friends.

◆ keyword

Lobbying
When people write to, or meet, MPs in order to campaign for changes in the law.

? questions

8. What would you suggest are the benefits of older and younger people coming together in this way?

9. Make a list of as many things as you can think of that are of concern to both young and old people alike.

10. What contribution do older people make to a project of this kind?

✳ coursework idea

If you have done any kind of voluntary work with older people there is an opportunity to reflect on what you did and the strengths and weaknesses of this to all involved.

Alternatively you may wish to talk to two older people who act as volunteers themselves, describing and assessing what they feel are the benefits of such work.

Older people are portrayed in the media in very different ways. Take two examples of this and critically compare the ways in which they are presented and the assumptions that are made about them.

Refugees

In this unit we look at the situation facing many refugees, particularly those who come to Britain. We look at the reasons why they have left their country of origin and ask what kind of treatment they should receive from the countries to which they have chosen to move.

Moving images

■ A sign of our times

Since 1990, there have probably been more refugees in the world than at any time in history. In 2001 it was estimated that about 23 million people were either refugees or displaced people in their own country. Explaining why this has happened is not easy.

Most people who become refugees leave their home or country because everyday life is almost impossible. Sometimes this is because of war, such as in Kosovo and Bosnia, part of the former Yugoslavia, where thousands of ordinary families were affected by the fighting.

When war takes place in a country where most people live in poverty, the problem becomes worse. Fighting stops the distribution of food. People leave to escape famine and serious outbreaks of disease. This was the case in Somalia in north east Africa in the late 1990s.

Many people who become refugees have been targeted because they belong to a particular ethnic or religious group. This has faced many Jewish people in the past and also now affects others – such as the Kurdish people in Iraq and Turkey.

? questions

1. What feelings do you have as you look at these pictures?

2. What do these pictures reveal about the kind of problems that refugees most often face? What other difficulties might refugees encounter?

■ Leaving home

Lian Hu Su lived in Beijing, the capital of China. In 1989 there were many protests against the Chinese government, which people felt was too harsh and brutal. Students, workers and many others took part in demonstrations telling the government that they should give people more freedom.

It was an offence to demonstrate against the government and to help anybody who was doing so. The army dealt with the protesters very severely.

Lian Hu Su felt the government was wrong and allowed some protestors to hide in his home. He was reported to the authorities. As the police were on their way to his flat, Lian Hu Su escaped.

Michaela is 20 years old. She lived with her family in a run-down town in Romania where, as a Roma Gypsy, she faced a lot of prejudice and discrimination. In 2002 she left Romania for a better life. 'Here you are very rich or very poor,' she said. 'My family, we have nothing. We live in a shack. Everyone has the right to seek happiness.'

Michaela's family paid for her to travel from Romania to France hidden in a lorry carrying soap powder. In Paris she hid under the carriage of a Eurostar train and was discovered by the police at Waterloo Station in London.

Shukri Ebrahim aged 15, lived with her family in Somalia, in north east Africa. There had been much fighting between government troops and different groups who were struggling for power. The government believed that Shukri's father was a member of one such group. One day three soldiers came to their house to take him away.

Shukri and her family were quite alone. She had no idea if the troops would come back and take the rest of the family, and could expect no help from her neighbours. Helping Shukri, they believed, would put themselves at risk. Shukri and her family decided they had to leave.

❓ questions

3. Why did each of the people in these stories leave their country? What other reasons do people have for leaving? Are any of these reasons more important than others?

4. In your opinion, does anyone have responsibility to help the people in each of these cases? If you think that they do, who has that responsibility and how far does it extend?

Refugees

War and peace

Much of British history has been shaped by those who have come to this country seeking war – and peace.

■ Invasion

From 55BC to 1066AD Romans, Angles, Saxons, Vikings and Normans came to invade and conquer Britain from all parts of Europe.

■ Safety

Others have come to Britain to *escape* war and violence. These range from the group of merchants from Armenia (a small country between Russia and Iran) who settled in Plymouth and London in the thirteenth century, to the families who came from Kosovo in 1999.

✳ facts

France Britain's reputation as a country offering safety to people who are being persecuted began with the arrival of the Huguenots from France. These were Protestants who were persecuted for their beliefs by the Roman Catholic Church in France for a period of more than a hundred years, between 1560 and 1685. Thousands died, but about 150,000 people escaped to safety in England, Ireland and America.

Russia Jewish communities have lived in Russia for 2,000 years. During this time they have faced periods of great persecution there and in many other countries.

? questions

1. What can other countries do when a government mistreats or fails to protect some of its citizens? What *should* they do?

2. In the nineteenth and early twentieth centuries there was no Jewish state of Israel, as there is now. Did anyone have a responsibility to help those who were being persecuted in Russia? If so, who, and for what reasons?

In 1835, the Czar (that is, the ruler of Russia), ordered all Jewish people to move to the western edge of the Russian empire. Much of this is now in Poland, Ukraine and Belarus. Restrictions were placed on where Jewish people could live, where they could travel and how they could earn a living. Jews were also often the first to be blamed for crimes, which they almost always had not committed.

In 1881, however, Czar Alexander II was assassinated, and one of those responsible was a Jewish woman. The result was an outbreak of violent attacks (called pogroms) on Jewish people throughout Russia. Thousands of Jews were slaughtered, often with the support and encouragement of the authorities. Groups were organised by the government to break up homes, destroy businesses, and even to kill members of hundreds of Jewish communities. The leaders of these groups were then publicly honoured. For their own safety, many Jewish families started to leave.

Between 1880 and 1910 about two million people left Russia for America, Germany, France, Britain and Australia.

■ Kosovo

The province of Kosovo used to be part of Yugoslavia, with local leaders having some control over their own affairs. This all changed with the break-up of Yugoslavia. From 1989 the mainly Albanian Muslim population of Kosovo was ruled by the government of the republic of Serbia, based in Belgrade, the former capital of Yugoslavia.

Most Kosovans believed they should be independent from Serbia. Most Serbs believed they should not. Kosovans protested about the unequal ways in which they were treated and some, who felt very strongly about this, formed the Kosovan Liberation Army and attacked and killed members of the Serbian forces in Kosovo.

The Serbian Government responded by killing many Kosovans and trying to drive others out of the country. The European Union, the United States and other countries started a military campaign against Serbia to stop this.

Ordinary Kosovan people suffered most. By 1999 the situation was very serious. In June of that year it was reported that there were about 860,000 Kosovan refugees who had left or been driven from their homes. About 4,000 were allowed to come to Britain. Others went to different countries. Within a year of the end of the war against Serbia, most refugees returned to Kosovo.

Podrimad Xheudet aged 29, was a teacher in Kosovo. He knew he was in danger from Serb forces where he lived, so he moved to Pristina, the capital of Kosovo. Soon Pristina came under attack and Podrimad moved on again with his family, looking for somewhere safe to stay. 'I had nothing,' he said. 'My house and my car were burned. My father and brothers were beaten.'

? questions

3. Why did Podrimad leave Kosovo and come to Britain?

4. What kind of responsibilities did the British Government have towards Podrimad and other refugees from Kosovo?

5. Did ordinary British people have any responsibilities towards the refugees who came from Kosovo? If so, what were they?

Refugees

Permission to stay

■ Going back or staying on?

Many people who seek safety abroad eventually return to settle in their own country. If those who wish to stay are not to be illegal immigrants they must apply for **asylum**.

When someone seeks asylum, they are asking to be officially recognised in that country as a refugee. If they are successful they will be allowed to stay on as a resident. If they are not, they will be deported.

■ Refugee status

Deciding whether a person can stay in a country permanently is a complicated process. In simple terms, immigration officials have to decide whether the person making the application fits a certain definition of the word 'refugee'. This is set out in the Convention Relating to the Status of Refugees, an international agreement passed by the United Nations in 1951, which most countries in the world have signed. It can be summarised as follows:

refugee \Ref`u*gee"\ n.

A refugee is a person who is outside their country and cannot return because of a well-founded fear of persecution for reasons of race, religion, nationality, membership of a particular social group or political opinion.

Someone whose situation does not meet the above test may still be allowed to stay, and be given, what is called Exceptional Leave to Remain. By special agreement they are allowed to stay in Britain if sending them home would seem to be very cruel or unkind.

Some people who seek asylum enter a country hoping to earn a better living for themselves and their family. This does not fit the definition of a refugee.

■ Waiting for a decision

Refugees who are waiting for a decision on their asylum claim are known as asylum seekers. Some refugees have their case dealt with quickly but many have had to wait several *years* for a decision. The Government is now trying to speed up the process.

? question

1. Put yourself in the position of someone who must decide whether each of the following people should be allowed to stay in this country.

   Look at the details of each case and decide whether they fit either of the tests above. If they do, the person should be granted refugee status and be allowed to stay. If not, they should be rejected and deported.

Muna's brother, along with 25 other army officers, was executed in 1990 for plotting to overthrow the government in Sudan. Muna helped to form an organisation to support the families of those who had been killed by government forces and was herself repeatedly arrested and threatened with rape. She came to England with her young daughter to stay with friends and then asked for asylum feeling that she could not face the continued danger any more.

Milan is a Roma from Slovakia. He asked for asylum for himself and his family in Britain after being attacked many times in Slovakia by skinheads. He said that there was a lot of prejudice against Roma people in Slovakia. 'We have words like "Gypsies to the gas chamber" daubed on our wall. We want to be free, but get no protection from the police.'

The British Government recognises that Roma people do have difficulties in Slovakia, but believes that the police there do provide some protection.

Sadiq's father was a politician in Iraq, and was critical of the government. One day, Sadiq was taken in for questioning. The soldiers wanted to know where his father was. He refused to tell them and was tortured. Sadiq's uncle managed to get him released by bribing his guards, but the questioning and beatings continued. Sadiq felt he had to leave. His father gave a trafficker £7,000 to get his son to the UK. Sadiq reached England in 12 days, hidden in a lorry with eight others.

Arif came to Britain as a refugee from Kosovo. While he was here, he became ill and was taken to hospital. Arif was told that he had a serious heart condition. He applied for asylum in Britain and asked not to be returned to Kosovo, because there were no medical facilities there that would properly deal with his illness.

 questions

2. Your teacher will give you details of the outcome of each of these cases. Are there any decisions that you disagree with? If so, explain why.

3. Some people try to come to Britain to escape from very poor living conditions in their own country. In many ways their lives are also in danger, but they don't fit the official definition of a refugee. Should they be allowed to stay in Britain? Give reasons for your answer.

keyword

Asylum
Seeking safety in another country when you are being persecuted for reasons of your race, religion, nationality, membership of a particular social group or political opinion.

Refugees

Modern times

■ Myth and reality

HANDOUT HUNTERS

We're allowing freeloaders into our small country when we have enough troubles with our own anti-social elements. The asylum laws should be immediately changed to ensure that we are not inundated with no-good people scurrying around the world looking for handouts.

A Thompson, Truro, Cornwall

ASYLUM CAMP

Should Britain keep taking immigrants? No, Britain does not have the space and economic capacity to absorb the same number it allowed in during the past 40 years. Walk in London and watch refugees thrusting babies at passers-by demanding money. I will not welcome other people here. We need a guarantee that if admitted, refugees will be returned when appropriate and no political asylum will be accepted.

J M Potton, Middlesex

■ The big picture

Refugees in Britain Details are given below of the numbers of people who asked for political asylum in Britain, 1998–2000.

You may have noticed that the numbers of people who were granted asylum added to those who were rejected does not equal the total figure of those who applied. This is because of the time it has taken for many people's asylum applications to be considered. Some of those who asked for asylum in 1998 did not have their case examined until 2000.

? questions

1. The above letters appeared in an English newspaper. Read them carefully and make a note of the points that the writers make about refugees.

2. Read through the rest of the information on these pages and check the accuracy of each of these points.

3. Finally, write a letter in reply to Ms Potton or Mr Thompson.

Refugees from Kosovo were taken to many parts of Britain. The banner over the door reads 'Welcome to Doncaster'.

Year	Numbers seeking asylum	Numbers granted asylum	Numbers allowed to stay temporarily	Numbers refused asylum
2000	80,315	10,375	11,495	72,015
1999	71,160	7,815	2,465	18,390
1998	46,015	5,345	3,910	22,315

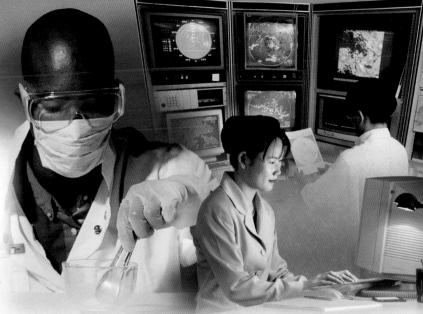

The waiting time now, however, is getting much shorter.

Taking the delays into account, 31 per cent of the people who applied to the UK for refugee status were allowed to stay in this country.

Another way of showing the number of refugees in the United Kingdom is to say that out of every 5,000 people in the UK, six are asylum-seekers and one will be allowed to stay.

Other countries The world's poorest countries have the greatest number of refugees. In 2001, Iran had 1.8 million refugees from Afghanistan and Pakistan a further 1.2 million. A year previously, nearly half a million people left Sierra Leone in West Africa for Guinea, Liberia, and Gambia.

Between 1991 and 2000, Germany received 1.7 million applications for political asylum. This was more than any other country in Europe. The UK received 428,000 applications over the same period.

However, in 2000, the UK received more asylum applications than any other country in Europe – although if this is looked at as a fraction of a country's population, the UK slips to number nine.

Costs Government figures show that the cost of dealing with applications from people seeking asylum in the United Kingdom steadily rose during the 1990s. The cost in 1999 was £475 million, rising to £590 million in 2000.

This represents one-fifth of one per cent of the amount we spend on health, benefits, education, police, defence etc.

Some people believe that asylum seekers come to this country just to obtain as much free support as possible. The rules state asylum seekers are not allowed to work in the first six months of their stay and may be provided with approximately £35 in money and vouchers. The Government announced in 2001 that the voucher system would be phased out and replaced with cash.

The Government wants to encourage highly skilled people to settle in Britain, but having a skill does not qualify an asylum seeker to be treated as a refugee. Some economists predict that over the next 25 years there will be a shortage of labour in this country, as the number of people of working age falls.

In the past, many refugees have made a great contribution to our economy and society – in business, education and the arts. Examples include Albert Einstein, Sigmund Freud and Karl Marx.

Many people who seek asylum in Britain already have skills and qualifications, for example in engineering and science. When they are eventually allowed to work, they all make a contribution to our economy.

coursework idea

Write a critical commentary on a newspaper report that covers the subject of refugees or asylum seekers.

81

Refugees

Refugees, aliens and asylum seekers

Huguenots arriving in Britain.

■ What's in a name?

Refugee is a French word, first used in Britain to describe the Huguenots fleeing from France over 400 years ago.
    Members of Jewish communities escaping from persecution in Russia more than 100 years ago were often referred to as *aliens*. The first laws passed to limit immigration to Britain at the beginning of the twentieth century were called the *Aliens Act* and *Aliens Order*.

■ Welcome to Britain

Many people facing persecution or danger in their own country have settled in Britain. But they have not always been made welcome.

In the news In 1888 the *Manchester City News* wrote of the refugees who were escaping from certain death in Russia.

> Their unclean habits, their wretched clothing and miserable food enable them to perpetuate existence upon a pittance. They have flooded the market with cheap labour.

In the 1930s, Jewish people again faced persecution. A large number of Jewish families tried to leave Germany, but at first were not always welcome in many countries, including Britain.

> Once it was known that Britain offered sanctuary to all who dared to come, the floodgates would be opened, and we would be inundated by thousands seeking a home.
>
> *Daily Mail 1935*

In recent years some people have again become concerned about the arrival of asylum seekers in Britain.
    This is how one newspaper described their arrival in Dover, Kent (population 55,000).

KOSOVANS, ALBANIANS AND YUGOSLAVIANS COME TO TOWN

FLOODGATES OPEN AGAIN TO REFUGEES

SOCIAL SERVICES were forced to use an emergency centre as 70 asylum seekers flooded into Dover. Poulton's Family Centre, in Folkestone Road, was opened on Friday evening after 35 Kosovan, Albanian and Yugoslavian refugees were discovered by immigration officers. The accommodation problem became even worse the following day with another 35 arrivals. They are the latest in a growing tide of asylum seekers flooding the area.

Local authorities are yet undecided...

? question

1. There are certain kinds of emotive words used in each of these extracts. What are they, and what pictures or images do they create? Why do you think they are used? What does the report *omit* to say about these refugees?

Seeking refuge

Taye, aged 17, left Ethiopia on false papers, with his mother and sister. They arrived in Britain and asked for asylum. Taye's father and brother had been taken from their house by troops. Taye and the rest of his family believed their lives were in danger, and fled.

'When we got off the plane at Heathrow my mother went to the police and said that we were asking for asylum. We were questioned by officials and taken to Manchester where we were given somewhere to stay.

'They said the house would be fully equipped, but we discovered when we arrived that we had just the basics. Three beds, some chairs and a table. There was no electricity for three days and it took three months for the gas to be connected. We had to buy many household items for ourselves from the £105 a week we were given, in money and vouchers for food.

'Our house was damp, because the roof leaked, and soon I started to suffer with asthma. I did not like to complain. It looked as if I was ungrateful and I was afraid that the landlord might evict us.'

British nationality

If an asylum seeker is allowed to stay here and work they may decide they want to remain permanently.

After three or, more usually, five years they may apply to become registered as a British citizen.

The main advantages of this are that they can obtain a British passport, vote and can stand for election.

The Government proposed at the beginning of 2002 that people who apply for British nationality should pass an English language test, study British society and make a citizenship pledge. The pledge would include an oath of loyalty to the Crown and an agreement to respect human rights and freedoms and democratic values.

? questions

2. What do refugees in Taye's position need? What should they be given?

3. How should we treat refugees who come to Britain? What rights should they have? Should refugees be given the same rights as other people living in Britain? At the moment they are entitled to fewer benefits than other people, they have little choice over where they live and have no rights against unfair eviction. Is this treatment fair? Give reasons for your answer.

4. Why do you think that some people feel that refugees are actually given *preferential* treatment?

? question

5. What arguments can you give for and against this suggestion? Which do you think are stronger?

Families

The first part of this unit looks at some of the different kinds of family arrangements we have in Britain today and asks whether governments should become involved in trying to change the way in which we live.

Changing times

Yesterday

Sheila and Patrick Callanan were married in 1953 and settled in north London. They soon started a family and, over the next 18 years, had a total of 12 children. This was unusually large by the standards of the 1960s and 1970s, but had been common in some communities in previous generations. Sheila and Patrick were married for just over 35 years, until Patrick died in 1989.

Today

Although they are all now in their thirties and forties and holding down good jobs, four of the Callanan clan still live in the family home and 11 of them gather weekly for Sunday lunch, cooked by their mother.

? question

1. What do you think are the advantages and disadvantages of this type of family arrangement?

Marriage

Six of the family have partners, five have married and three have children. Through their own choice most have decided to remain single or not yet marry – reflecting current trends towards later marriage, smaller families and independent living.

? question

2. Why do you think many younger people today have, like some of the Callanans, chosen to stay independent or to live together and not to marry?

Traditional families: image or reality?

The Callanans are what is known as an extended family. More common is the nuclear family of two married parents living with their children at the same address, and often some distance from close relations. This is just one example of the different forms of family patterns that we have today.

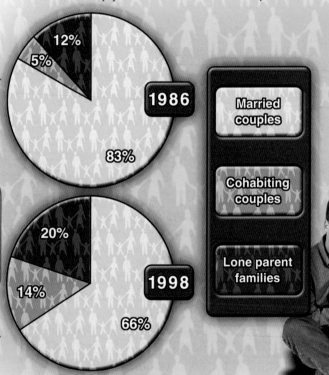

1986: 12%, 5%, 83%
1998: 20%, 14%, 66%

Married couples
Cohabiting couples
Lone parent families

? questions

3. What changes do you notice in family arrangements between 1986 and 1998?

4. Suggest and explain one positive and one negative consequence of the move away from the traditional nuclear family.

Explaining family diversity

Family patterns today can vary a great deal. They may be led by a single adult, based on cohabitation (living together) rather than marriage, or be a step family containing parents or children from more than one family. Some reasons for these changes are set out below.

Marriage More people are deciding to delay marriage (particularly those who spend longer in education) or not to marry at all. People who marry later tend to have smaller families.

Contraception Advances in contraception have granted women greater control over when, whether and with whom they have children.

Employment Changes at work and in the home have led to women gaining more financial and social independence from men. This means that they may be less inclined to stay in an unhappy relationship.

Women who want a career tend to have fewer children and take less time out from work.

Tolerance Changing attitudes to homosexuality have seen the emergence of more families led by gay couples and single gay people.

Divorce Separation and divorce have become more commonplace and are no longer stigmatised in the way that they once were. As separation and divorce have grown, so has remarriage, making step families increasingly common.

Back to basics

Some people regret the decline of the traditional family and the growth of other types of family arrangements. For moral, religious or cultural reasons, they stress the importance of a child living with two parents who are married to one another, and believe that this arrangement works for the benefit of the individual and for society as a whole.

During the early 1990s the Conservative Prime Minister, John Major, called for a 'back to basics' crusade in all areas of life, especially the family. In the late 1990s, both the Conservative and new Labour governments proposed new laws designed to encourage couples seeking a divorce to obtain counselling and guidance and so improve the chances of them staying together.

The legislation did not come into force and rather than 'rescue' the traditional family, the crusade served only to draw press attention to the complicated personal lives of a number of public figures. Nonetheless, government policy continues to encourage 'family values'.

ONE-THIRD OF MARRIAGES NOW END DIVORCE!

NEW GOVERN
shown that the fa
is still on the in
The results of
the divorce r
risen to a po
couples ent
themselve

? questions

5. Research shows that family tensions can have a damaging effect on children, and on society in general. Does the Government have responsibility to encourage parents to marry and live with their children in a traditional way – or are these personal matters in which it has no right to intervene? Explain your answer.

6. There is a wide variety of family patterns in the United Kingdom today. How do responsibilities, roles and patterns of behaviour vary in families you know?

The second part of this unit looks at the questions of abuse and violence in the family.

Abuse and violence

■ Hidden crime

In 2000, the National Society for the Prevention of Cruelty to Children (NSPCC) asked nearly 3,000 young adults about their experiences of childhood. More than nine out of ten reported that their family life as a child had been a warm and happy time.

A minority, however, had suffered significant abuse and neglect. This included being hit or even burnt by a parent or carer, threats, humiliation, violence between parents, neglect and sexual abuse.

Help

ChildLine, Kidscape and the NSPCC are specialist organisations that provide helplines and websites offering advice and counselling for children and young people.

ChildLine
0800 1111
www.childline.org.uk

kidscape
020 7730 3300

NSPCC
Cruelty to children must stop. FULL STOP.
www.nspcc.org.

? questions

1. What do you understand is the difference between neglect and abuse?

2. What do you imagine are the effects of abuse or neglect of children on the victim and on the wider family unit?

■ Smacking children: whose right?

A survey undertaken by the Government in 2000 showed that nine out of ten people in England and Wales were in favour of the right of parents to smack their child. However, a year earlier, another study found that 73 per cent favoured a ban, as long as parents were not prosecuted for minor smacks.

'If a parent cannot slipper a child, the world is going potty.' *Judge Ian McLean*

'This Labour Government believes in parental discipline. Smacking has a part in that. Our law will do nothing to outlaw smacking.'

Paul Boateng MP, when he was Minister for Health

'Smacking children is morally wrong. If people are smacked a lot it's bound to cause problems. But I don't think it should be a punishable offence. That would be an invasion of individual rights.' *Si Piwko, parent*

'There's a big difference between smacking, hitting and beating. There's no harm in a little slap given at the right time for the right reason.' *Dannii Fortune, parent*

3. What are the arguments for and against parents smacking their children?

4. Why do some see the smacking of children as a slippery slope that leads to an acceptance of violence in the family?

5. What do you think Si Piwko means when he says that punishment for smacking would be an 'invasion of individual rights'?

United Kingdom?

England As the law stands today, parents, babysitters and child minders each have the right to hit a child in their care, as long as the punishment is 'moderate and reasonable'. The Government has no plans to change the law.

Wales and Northern Ireland Consultations are under way to decide whether a change in the law is desirable.

Scotland A new law is proposed to prevent anyone hitting a child under the age of three.

? question

6. Where do you think the law should stand on the physical punishment of children? Explain your views.

Domestic violence

Research in 1999 revealed that 30 murders occur each year in London because of domestic violence. The study also showed that:

- one woman in four experiences domestic violence
- an allegation of domestic violence is made to police in London every 12 minutes
- on 90 per cent of the occasions when domestic violence occurs, children are in the same or the next room.

Campaigners against domestic violence paint a similar picture nationally and argue that this type of violence occurs in every community and all social classes.

? questions

7. How would you define domestic violence?

8. What are the difficulties in discovering the truth about violence in the family?

9. Some people have said that more steps should be taken to prevent family violence. Suggestions include help for families facing these difficulties, education about the issue in schools and setting up a register of people who have committed domestic violence or abuse.

What are the strengths and weaknesses of each of these measures?

The law

Hitting someone or threatening to do so is a criminal offence, and the police may charge the violent person if there is sufficient evidence.

A court can also order one partner to stop assaulting or threatening the other and can order that person to leave the home. If the violent partner breaks the court order (called an injunction), the victim may call the police or go back to court and ask for that person to be sent to prison. It is important for a person in this situation to obtain legal advice.

If a victim of domestic violence leaves home to seek help, the council must provide temporary accommodation if the victim is in danger and homeless.

Education

This unit looks at the questions of rights and responsibilities in education. The first part focuses on exclusion from school and asks 'how important is a person's right to education?'

Bullies

Michelle's story

Michelle lives in a large town on the South coast. She is an easy-going sort of person, but has no real interest in school, and feels that she achieves very little when she does attend.

Michelle suffered a period of bullying in Years 8 and 9. She told her mum who eventually reported the matter to school. Four girls were mainly responsible. They were seen by the head, Mrs Rogers, and the problem finally seemed to go away. However, while all this was going on, Michelle had got into the habit of not going to school and this continued after the issue had been sorted out.

Michelle is now in Year 11 and her attendance continues to be poor.

? questions

1. Michelle is losing out on her right to education. From what you have read of her case, who might have responsibility for this?

2. How serious a problem do you think bullying is?

3. What do you think is the best way to tackle bullying and other disruptive behaviour?

■ The head's problem

Michelle believes that her accent was probably the reason why she was picked on. She could just about take the name calling, but the worst thing was when the girls used to tip her bag out and go through all her stuff, holding up each item for everyone to see. They just humiliated her.

When Mrs Rogers spoke to the people responsible, she pointed out that their behaviour was not acceptable and was damaging Michelle's education. She told the girls they would be excluded if it continued.

? question

4. What are the arguments for and against the head teacher excluding these girls?

■ Exclusion headache

Too easy? Exclusions from schools rose sharply in the years up to 1997, to nearly 13,000 a year. Part of this increase, some people said, was caused by the new league tables of exam results, as schools excluded trouble-some students in order to keep up their overall pass rate.

Many of the excluded students were not being educated elsewhere. Some would hang around the streets during school hours committing crime.

In response to this, the Government decided to make it harder for schools to exclude pupils and, by the end of 2001, exclusions had fallen to just over 8,000 a year.

Simranjit

> IT'S NOT **GOOD** THAT BULLIES ARE ALLOWED BACK INTO SCHOOL. THEY COULD JUST PICK **ANOTHER** VICTIM.

Too hard? Some heads complained that they were unable to exclude some pupils who really deserved it. Immediate exclusion was allowed only on grounds of sexual misconduct, drug dealing or serious violence (actual or threatened).

In 2002 the Secretary of State announced that schools would also be able to exclude pupils on-the-spot for carrying weapons or 'serious' bullying.

Marlene

> IF THEY ARE GONE FOREVER IT MIGHT NOT BE THAT GOOD BECAUSE THEY WILL CARRY ON **OUTSIDE** OF SCHOOL. YOU CAN PUNISH THEM AND THEY WILL KNOW NOT TO DO IT AGAIN. AT LEAST IN SCHOOL THERE ARE **TEACHERS** AROUND TO STOP IT.

? questions

5. What kind of bullying do you think is serious enough to deserve immediate exclusion?

6. Is it right for the Government to lay down strict rules for excluding pupils or should it be left to individual schools to decide what is right for them?

7. What rights should parents have about the education of their children?

? question

8. Whose views are you more sympathetic towards? Why?

■ Fair treatment?

If a head teacher excludes a pupil for more than five days in a term, the governors have to decide whether to support or overrule the exclusion. The views of parents must be listened to and in more serious cases excluded pupils can also attend the meeting to give their side of the story. Parents have the right to appeal against the governors' ruling to an appeal panel set up by the local authority.

■ Opinion

Here are some views of students.

Minak

> EXPELLING **BULLIES** WILL HELP EVERYONE, NOT JUST THE ONE WHO WAS BEING BULLIED, BY HELPING US **CARRY ON** WITH OUR EDUCATION.

? question

9. Should someone who bullies another person expect to be treated fairly, even if they have not treated others in the same way?

Education

The right to education

■ Malcolm

Malcolm is African-Caribbean British and lives on a large housing estate in a run down area of London.

A lot of the adults who live on the estate are unemployed, especially the men. Malcolm did well at primary school but at secondary school things were different. For a combination of reasons, Malcolm found himself getting into more and more trouble with the teachers and unable to settle down to work for his GCSEs. He was given a series of **fixed-term exclusions** but these only made it harder for him to feel at home in the school. Eventually teachers decided that his behaviour had become so bad that he was permanently excluded.

? questions

1. What factors do you think might contribute to people like Malcolm being excluded from school?

2. How far might it be true to say that Malcolm only has himself to blame for his exclusion?

3. What impact will it have on his future if Malcolm leaves school with few or no GCSEs?

■ Excluded from school and society

When the Labour Party was elected to government in 1997 it set up a special unit to look at levels of what it called 'social exclusion'.

Social exclusion describes the situation of people who don't get a fair share of the benefits that society has to offer.

They are probably on low income, which means that they are more likely to suffer ill health, more likely to be the victims of crime, less likely to do well at school and so on. If Malcolm fails to get any qualifications, he himself could become stuck in a cycle of this kind, believing that he has nothing to offer himself or society.

■ An educated workforce

In order to compete economically with other countries, Britain needs a workforce that is skilled and well educated.

? question

4. Why is it good for society as a whole for governments to try to reduce the number of people out of work and on low income?

Lifelong learning

Years ago it tended to be harder for people like Malcolm, who did not succeed at school, to have another opportunity to get a good education. Today, the Government encourages people to think of learning as something that happens throughout life.

Alice has just passed her seventh GCSE – at the age of 81. She began to study when she retired from her job as a bus conductor because she felt that she had never really had the chance to pass any exams. Each year she takes a new course.

David is 21 and is in his second year at university, taking a degree in German and Russian. He works part-time in a restaurant to help pay for his course. He'd like to work as an interpreter.

Mehmet comes from Cyprus, but has been living in Britain for over 30 years. At first he worked in a bottle factory, but when he lost his job he decided to try to go to college to train as an engineer. Mehmet is now a control room manager in a modern power station.

Paula left school without any GCSEs. She became interested in child care helping at her daughter's playgroup, and decided that she wanted to be trained properly. She eventually became a regional organiser for the Playgroups Association and is now taking a degree in child development. She hopes to become a college lecturer.

? questions

5. How important is it that each of these people has the chance to learn new skills? Who benefits from their improved education?

6. Each person described above has had to pay for their education themselves. Alice pays a pound a week. Mehmet and Paula have each paid about £3,000 for their training. At the end of his course, David will be about £8,000 in debt.

   Should education for people after they have left school be free of charge to whoever wants it? Think of arguments for and against this idea.

7. Governments often place education high on their lists of priorities (compared with, say, social services). How far do you agree with this? What education issues are currently in the news?

❖ keywords

Fixed-term exclusion
Exclusion from school for a set length of time, which may not be for more than 45 days in a school year.

Student voice

No council here

Bernard Jones is headteacher of a comprehensive school in Oxford. He is a good head, liked by the pupils and respected by the staff. When thinking about changes to the school, he always makes a point of consulting widely before doing anything. With just over 700 students the school is not particularly large. Mr Jones prides himself on knowing every student by name.

'I make myself available to students every lunchtime,' said Mr Jones. 'I am out and about in the school. Pupils can always come up to me and tell me what's on their minds.'

Surprisingly, perhaps, Mr Jones is against school councils. He thinks that too often school councils do not work and can give pupils the wrong idea about democracy. 'The one thing adolescents can spot a mile off is hypocrisy and I reckon schools typically are full of hypocrisy. The words don't fit the music. They say one thing and immediately do another. There are limits to the powers of school councils. I and my deputies see all students personally once a year and I give them a chance to tell me if they would like to see anything changed.'

? questions

1. How far do you agree with Mr Jones's views? Discuss the advantages and disadvantages of his system of giving students a direct voice.

Student councils

Recent research has found that about half of all secondary schools in England and Wales have school councils – and the number is rising. Many primary schools also have councils, some involving Year 1 children.

Stile Way School in Cheshire has 1,900 students. The school is divided into six houses, each with a student council. Each house council sends one student to the main school council, which also includes the head, teaching and non-teaching staff, a parent and a governor.

Recent questions for discussion:
• What new lunchtime and after school clubs would you like to see in school?
• It has been suggested that the vending machine is stocked with Pot Noodles. Would this be acceptable?
• What measures can you suggest for improving the state of the school toilets?
• The school council has £400 to spend. How should it be used?

Organisation In most schools, one representative from each form is elected to the council. In large schools this means that it can be made up of at least 50 students. Some schools feel this is too many and have adopted a two-tier council with house or class groups reporting to a smaller full council.

Havenden Community College in Sussex has 2,000 students. Every form elects a representative who sits on the school council, which is made up of more than 60 students. Two teachers also attend.

Recent questions for discussion
• What are your opinions of recent changes in the school day?
• How can students become more involved in selecting senior staff?
• Who will represent the school on the town's youth council?
• Where is the best place to locate the new Year 10 base?

? questions

2. Compare and contrast these two school councils, including the way that they are made up and the business they deal with.

3. One student said of the council in her school, 'We can complain until we're blue in the face about our limited choice of options or the lack of good sex and drugs education, but we're not really taken seriously unless we're talking about things like locks on the toilet doors and toilet rolls.'

   Why is this student critical of the council? What steps might improve the situation?

4. What aspects of school life do you consider worth reviewing in your own school?

■ Is there a right to be heard?

Britain has signed the United Nations Convention on the Rights of the Child. Article 12 of this document sets out the right of 'the child who is capable of forming his or her own views to express those views freely in all matters affecting the child'. The document says that these views should be 'given due weight in accordance with the age and maturity of the child'.

? questions

5. In the light of the UN Convention, discuss the view that all schools (primary and secondary) should be required to have a school council of some kind.

6. Are there any issues that should never be discussed by a school council? If so, what are they and why?

7. Make a list of the different groups in your area affected by the way your school is run. Do any of these have a right to be consulted. If so, who, and why?

Managing the economy

This unit explains some of the decisions governments have to take when running the nation's economy.

Moving target

One of the most important things that a government has to do is to manage the economy of the country.

Most governments would probably like their country to be prosperous, with plenty of work for everyone, stable prices and money for hospitals, schools and other public services. But this is not easy to achieve. One reason is that the economy of a country is always in a state of flux or change.

■ The business cycle

Boom, recession and recovery are words often used to describe a country's economic position. They refer to the fact that, over a period of time, most businesses and industries go through a cycle of change.

During a *boom* things are going well. Businesses have full order books. They invest in new equipment, employ more workers and many people have more money. However, sooner or later a number of problems emerge. Costs tend to rise pushing up prices – so that eventually people decide not to buy some of the goods and services on offer

The economy then tends to slow down and may move into a period of *recession*. A fall in demand means that businesses can't sell all the things that they make or provide. They buy fewer supplies and then start to lay off some of their workers. Some firms will close down.

Eventually, business confidence begins to return. The *recovery* can take several years, but investment gradually increases and new jobs are created. The economy moves once again on an upward cycle.

Means of control

Governments today usually try to minimise the effects of this cycle and do their best to avoid sharply rising prices (called inflation) and large-scale unemployment.

Two ways in which this is done are through a) *taxation* and b) *government spending*.

Raising taxes tends to reduce the amount that people spend, but enables governments to spend more on public services. Increasing government spending eventually puts money into the economy by creating more jobs and giving some people more spending power.

■ Taxation

People in Britain pay taxes – that is money to the government – in several ways.

Direct taxes are taxes on incomes and savings – and, for businesses, taxes on profits. Direct taxes are paid proportionately. Generally speaking, the more a person earns above a certain level, the more they pay in tax.

Indirect taxes are taxes on spending. The largest of these is VAT (value added tax), which is charged at 17.5 per cent on almost all goods and services that we buy. Some products, such as fuel, alcohol and tobacco, are taxed further and these extra duties form an important part of a government's income.

Social security: benefits
£104,000 million

Education: school, colleges,
universities
£21,000 million

Health: hospitals, doctors,
medical services
£52,000 million

Defence: the armed forces
£24,000 million

International aid: helping
poorer countries
£3,000 million

Law and order: police
and prisons
£9,000 million

? questions

1. People who are on low and medium incomes usually pay a maximum of 20 per cent of their income in tax. Those on high incomes pay 40 per cent. Would it be fairer if everybody paid the same? Explain your views.

2. Some people feel we should pay less tax, others believe it should be more. What are the arguments for and against these views?

Government spending One of the ways in which governments manage the economy is by deciding exactly how much of the money it raises in taxes will be spent on public services.

Spending money on roads, schools and hospitals creates more jobs and puts money back into the economy. Too much government spending at the wrong time, however, tends to lead to inflation.

▮ Choices

The Chancellor of the Exchequer, the government minister with responsibility for finance, has to decide how much money will be raised by taxes and how much can then be spent on public services.

Big spenders? In 2002 approximately £350,000 million was set aside to pay for public services and other kinds of government spending. The pie chart (above, right) shows where some of this money was spent.

? questions

3. Does anything surprise you about these figures? If so, what is it, and why?

4. Each year the government decides on its spending priorities. Imagine that these are the main proposals for the coming year.

    - Increase numbers in the **police** force.
    - Improve **housing** in the run-down parts of our major cities.
    - Increase the **defence** budget to combat the threat of world terrorism.
    - Improve **social security** benefits for the very poor.
    - Build more **motorways**.
    - Improve the **rail** service.
    - Build more **hospitals**.
    - Increase UK **aid** to poorer parts of the world.

    Which four would you nominate as the most valuable? Why? (You may wish to add a proposal that is not on this list.)

5. If the government can't afford all of these, can you suggest any other ways in which they might be paid for?

Governing ourselves

This unit looks at some of the recent changes in the way that we are governed.

A United Kingdom?

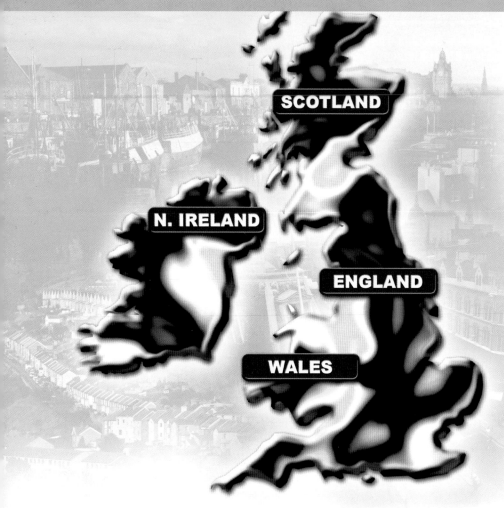

SCOTLAND

N. IRELAND

ENGLAND

WALES

The United Kingdom achieved its present form in 1922 when southern Ireland separated from the north, leading to the creation of an independent Republic of Ireland.

Differences and similarities

Today the United Kingdom has three separate court and legal systems. England and Wales have one; Scotland and Northern Ireland each have another.

The main law-making body, however, remains Parliament, based in London.

Devolution

Devolution means passing authority from central to regional government. In the United Kingdom there is now devolved government in Northern Ireland, Scotland and Wales.

The New Northern Ireland Assembly
A devolved parliament was created in Northern Ireland in 1922, but was abolished in the early 1970s because of the conflict between Protestant and Catholic groups.

In 1998, following the Good Friday Agreement, the New Northern Ireland Assembly was established. It has 108 elected members and has the power to decide on matters of health, social services, environment, education and agriculture that affect the people of Northern Ireland. These arrangements are designed to make sure that both Catholics and Protestant share in the decision-making process.

The United Kingdom is made up of England, Northern Ireland, Scotland and Wales. It hasn't always been like this. At one stage the countries were quite separate. It wasn't until 1536 that Wales was formally united with England. Union with Scotland took place in 1707, and in 1800, there was union with Ireland.

Union, however, is probably not the word that people in Ireland, Scotland or Wales would have used at the time to describe their new link with England. The 'union' was dominated by England, with power and influence largely resting in London.

The National Assembly for Wales, Cardiff

The National Assembly for Wales In 1997 a referendum was held in Wales proposing devolution. The 'yes' vote was just large enough to enable a National Assembly for Wales to be created in 1999. Its 60 elected members make decisions about some local issues affecting the people of Wales. However, all laws passed by Parliament in Westminster still apply to Wales.

The Scottish Parliament In the 1960s and 1970s an increasing number of people began to support the idea of greater independence for Scotland. A devolution referendum held in 1979 did not get enough support, but when another was held in 1997, people in Scotland gave a clear 'yes' to the creation of their own new parliament.

The Scottish Parliament opened in Edinburgh in 1999. The 129 Members of the Scottish Parliament (MSPs) have the power to pass laws affecting domestic policy in Scotland, but matters of foreign affairs, defence and economic policy continue to be decided by Parliament in London.

? questions

1. What do you believe are the advantages to people in Northern Ireland, Wales and Scotland of devolution? Are there any possible drawbacks? If so, what might they be?

2. 'If Wales, Scotland and Northern Ireland have their own Assembly or Parliament, England should have one also.' What do you think are the strengths and weaknesses of this idea?

The city mayor

The attack on the Twin Towers in New York on 11 September 2001 brought Rudolph Giuliani to the attention of the world. New Yorkers knew him well. He had been their city mayor for eight years. He hadn't always been popular, but he did have a reputation for tough talking, and for getting things done. Even his strongest political critics agreed that his leadership in the weeks after the attack was quite exceptional.

One of his other major achievements was to turn New York from the murder capital of the world to one of the safest cities in America. Under his direction there was a 62 per cent drop in crime – the steepest fall for 30 years.

Good for all? The Government is strongly encouraging cities in Britain to elect their own mayor, with increased powers to manage their area. Londoners elected Ken Livingstone as their first mayor in 2000. Those in favour of the idea see it as a way of getting more people interested in local politics and giving them a say in how things are done. Putting one person in charge makes it much harder for excuses to be offered when things go wrong and promises are not kept.

Not everyone agrees, however. There was much opposition in Birmingham to an elected mayor. 'Putting one person in charge of a £2 million budget would be a disaster,' said one councillor. 'Would they really be interested in emptying bins and filling holes in the road?'

? questions

3. What do you feel about the idea of having a local city mayor? What do you think are the strengths and weaknesses of the idea?

The power of the media

This unit looks at the influence of the media on our lives and asks whether there should be any changes in the way that it operates.

The front page

Almost every newspaper puts its main story on the front page. It is the section of the paper, apart perhaps from the sport, where most readers look first. It can also determine whether people choose to buy the newspaper.

The decision about which of the big stories a newspaper will use, and where they will go, is taken each day by a small group of their senior journalists, including the editor.

A sample of the news on one day in May 2002.

FRANCE Marches throughout France protesting against the far-right leader Jean Marie Le Pen.

CRIME Government plans to withdraw benefits from parents of persistent young offenders.

AFGHANISTAN UK troops in major Afghan offensive.

POP Claim that **Britney Spears** is not a virgin.

RACE The comedian at a Leeds United awards dinner makes a string of racist jokes.

SPORT Report that the England team will take Jaffa Cakes with them to the **2002 World Cup**

POLITICS ARTICLE URGING READERS NOT TO VOTE FOR THE EXTREME RIGHT-WING BNP IN THE FORTHCOMING ELECTION.

DRUGS Britain's Chief Constables call for users of hard drugs not to be prosecuted but sent for treatment instead.

? questions

1. Put yourself in the position of the people deciding which stories their newspaper should use. Are there any on the list that you feel should not be included?

2. Many papers today put three stories on the front page. Which three from the list above would *you* select? Which story would you place first? What criteria did you use in reaching this decision?

3. The articles that you selected above show something about the kind of job that you think a newspaper should be doing. What is the purpose of a newspaper? Explain your views.

▦ In the know

There are very few people whose job places them at the centre of events. Most of us learn what is happening through the media – newspapers, radio, television, and more recently the Internet.

This places people who either own or work for the media in a powerful position – giving them a huge influence on how people interpret world events.

MAIN SOURCE OF WORLD NEWS

Newspapers 16%
Radio 14%
Television 66%

Source: Public View 2001

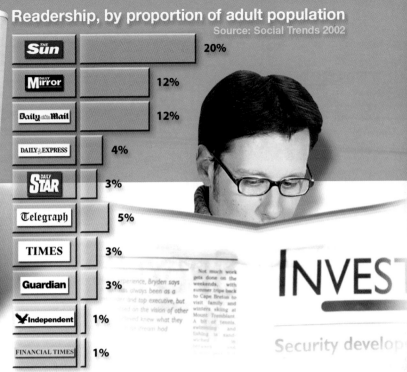

Readership, by proportion of adult population

Source: Social Trends 2002

Newspaper	Percentage
The Sun	20%
Daily Mirror	12%
Daily Mail	12%
Daily Express	4%
Daily Star	3%
Telegraph	5%
TIMES	3%
Guardian	3%
Independent	1%
FINANCIAL TIMES	1%

Television The main source of world and national news for most people in Britain is the television, although newspapers are more important for local news.

Newspapers More than half the adult population read a newspaper every day. The *Sun* is the most popular.

? question

4. In 2002, for the first time, more than half of the UK's television viewers had access to multi-channel television. If this trend continues, most of the population will soon have 50 or 100 channels at their disposal. Some programmes, on BBC World and CNN, will be seen by people throughout the world – others, on minority issues, will have a tiny audience.

   What do you imagine will be the advantages and disadvantages of such changes?

■ Ownership and control

Television The BBC began broadcasting radio programmes in 1922. Television transmission started in 1936, but was suspended with the outbreak of war in 1939. BBC programmes are financed through the annual licence fee that must be paid, with some exceptions, by every household with a television set.

Independent Television (ITV) came into existence in 1955. The terrestrial channels 3,4 and 5 are funded through advertising, and cable and satellite services through subscription.

Newspapers Newspapers are commercial ventures. They depend for their survival on making money for their owners and shareholders. Most of the national newspapers in Britain (87 per cent of sales) are produced by four companies. The largest, News International, owns the *Sun*, *The Times*, the *Sunday Times* and the *News of the World* and has a 37 per cent market share.

? question

5. Over the last 30 years a relatively small group of companies has taken control of large sections of the media in Britain. It is now common for newspaper groups also to own a significant share of independent radio and television stations.

   What are the advantages and disadvantages of this situation?

The power of the media
Managing the news

Somewhere in Britain

During the Second World War many towns and cities in Britain were heavily bombed. Whilst those who were directly affected knew exactly what was going on, certain information was always kept from the public at large. Pictures and details of bomb damage were deliberately kept of out the papers for fear of giving information to the enemy and lowering public morale.

Most people are prepared to accept a certain degree of censorship at times of war, but is there a point at which it becomes unacceptable?

Bomb damage after an air raid on London, 1940. Photographs like this were not published until the war had ended.

How far do you go?

After the September 11 attacks on New York and Washington, the British and American governments asked the media in both countries to limit broadcasts of Osama Bin Laden and his associates, who praised the attacks and warned that more would follow.

A spokesperson for the American president said that broadcasting propaganda statements from the man held responsible for the deaths of more than 5,000 people could not be in the interests of the United States.

The material, he said, might encourage some people to volunteer to fight with the Taliban and could also contain hidden codes ordering further attacks on the West.

Some people thought that this approach was a mistake. They believed that if Osama Bin Laden and his group wanted to communicate with followers

there were many other ways in which they could do it – such as via the Internet or by mobile phone.

They also said that the real reason for this censorship was both governments' fear that publicity for Osama Bin Laden and the Taliban could reduce support for the war against them.

 **questions**

1. The difficulties of deciding whether or not to censor the Taliban film was discussed at great length on the Internet. Here are three extracts from messages published on the BBC site.

> **>Phil H, UK**
>
> 'By showing these tapes, the media are acting as pawns in Osama Bin Laden's campaign.'

> **>C.Meyer, US**
>
> 'Not to censor these tapes would be extremely short-sighted and ultimately irresponsible.'

> **>Safarali Senego, India**
>
> 'Let the truth be told. Do not give to the people only the western or eastern version of the truth.'

How do you respond to each of these points? On balance, what action would you recommend?

■ The role of the media

In 1988 Independent Television made a programme called *Death on the Rock*, investigating the circumstances surrounding the death of three members of the IRA (the Irish Republican Army), shot by the SAS (Special Air Service) in Gibraltar.

Since the 1970s, members of the IRA had carried out terrorist attacks in Northern Ireland and on the UK mainland.

Despite strong pressure from the Government, the programme was broadcast. Margaret Thatcher, Prime Minister at the time, complained that the media provided terrorists with 'the oxygen of publicity.'

More recently, certain sections of the press have been criticised for failing to support wholeheartedly the war in Afghanistan.

? question

2. What do you feel should be the role of the media in time of war?

■ How far do you go?

News reports rarely give just the basic facts. The emphasis, the choice of subject, and the language used are all subtle influences on the reader.

By choosing to put the story about the racist comedian on its front page (see page 98), the *Daily Mirror* was deliberately emphasising the unacceptability of racist language.

When the *Daily Mail* reports on Labour's tax plans 'to savage high earners', it carries the message that this (at least as far as the paper and its owners are concerned) is a mistake and thoroughly unfair.

Sometimes the process of managing the news is taken a stage further by those who are creating it.

When Mrs Thatcher wanted to draw attention to the need to clear our towns and cities of litter, her staff arranged for papers and cans to be *deliberately* dropped on the grass in a London park so that the Prime Minister could be photographed doing something about the problem by picking them up!

Another example of an attempt at news management was the message sent to colleagues by a British government adviser shortly after the second plane hit the World Trade Center in New York on September 11. 'It's now a very good day to get out anything we want to bury. Councillors' expenses? – Jo.'

? questions

3. How was the government adviser attempting to manage the news after the tragedy in New York?

4. 'There's nothing wrong with governments wanting to put themselves in the best light. It's quite natural. Everyone does it.' How would you reply to this view?

5. Finally you might like to look at the evidence of bias in this unit on the media. What kinds of messages do you think the authors are trying to give?

The power of the media

Freedom to publish

This topic discusses whether limits should be placed on what appears in the media.

Violence There is concern that violence in the media desensitises us to the horrors of injury and suffering and encourages some people to copy the things that they hear, read or see on the screen. Violence is often represented as a way of resolving problems. Why not, critics argue, place greater emphasis on discussion, co-operation and compromise?

Some research has shown a connection between viewing habits and violent behaviour, but other work questions this. One of the difficulties in making a link is that anti-social behaviour is the result of many factors, and not only exposure to media violence.

Sex Until the 1960s the American film industry followed what was known as the Hays Production Code. This was an agreement that film makers were required to follow setting out what could and could not be shown. 'Excessive and lustful kissing' was forbidden and when a man and woman were pictured on a couch, each was required to have one foot on the floor.

Film and television today would be very different if the Code was still in force. A survey carried out in 1999 for the British Broadcasting Standards Commission said that people were becoming more tolerant of sex on television, but the coverage of sex in some soaps and in daytime talk shows was thought by many to be unacceptable. Women and older people were more likely to be critical of the portrayal of sex on TV.

■ Number one

In 2001 Eminem received four nominations for the prestigious music industry's Grammy awards. Outside the Staples Center in Los Angeles, where the ceremony was held, hundreds of protestors gathered to demonstrate about his songs.

The violent and obscene content of the lyrics and anti-women and anti-gay sentiments have led people to call for his music to be banned. One album describes a rape fantasy and murder.

However, not everyone is offended. 'I don't think people will go out and start beating and killing people because of this album,' said one singer. Others defended Eminem's right to freedom of expression.

? question

1. How do you react to this problem? Would you place any limits on a singer's freedom of expression? If so why, and what would they be?

? question

2. It is often said that if a person doesn't like what they see on television, they can always turn it off. How far do you agree with this argument? To what extent does it deal with the criticisms that are made about sex and violence on television?

■ Private lives

When radio presenter Sara Cox left for her honeymoon in the Seychelles she did not expect that pictures of her and her husband naked by the pool at their villa would be shown in a Sunday newspaper. A photographer had rented the house next door to where the couple were staying, specifically to take the pictures.

Sara Cox claimed that this was an unreasonable invasion of her privacy.

Privacy Anyone who believes that their privacy has been invaded by the press may take their complaint to the Press Complaints Commission – a body run by the newspaper industry. If the Commission finds that the complaint is reasonable, it will order the newspaper to publish an apology.

The standard test in cases of this kind is whether the information revealed by the newspaper is *'in the public interest'*.

Additionally, the person concerned may take their case to court – either to obtain an order banning publication or to seek damages. However, this can be expensive and beyond many people's means.

Some complainants have now started to use the *Human Rights Act* (see pages 20–21), asserting their right to respect for their private life.

Balance A difficulty here is the balance between press freedom and respect for privacy. Too many restrictions prevent newspapers and television reporting important information. Too few allow an unreasonable intrusion

(see pages 20–21)

? question

3. Look at the following cases and decide whether you think that publication is acceptable. Explain your thinking in each case.

- The ex-boyfriend of a Coronation Street star sells his account of their life together to a newspaper. This includes intimate details of their sex life, which the paper publishes.

- A Premiership footballer, married with two children, has affairs with two women who both sell their stories to a newspaper. The footballer asks a court to order that his name should not be published.

- On a trip to a remote part of Chile, in his year between school and university, Prince William is photographed hiking and crossing a river. The pictures are published in a British magazine.

- A television personality visits a female prostitute, who sells the story to a newspaper. The man tries to stop the story being published.

Left: Until he was 18, the press agreed not to publish pictures of Prince William without the permission of the Royal Family.

Voting and elections

This unit looks at the different ways in which people can vote and asks if parts of our voting system should be changed.

A problem for the Council

Labour councillors in Bristol had a problem. The cost of providing **public services** in the city was going up and up. The biggest expense was education. Like most other councils, Bristol spends more on education than on anything else.

To continue to provide people in Bristol with the level of education services that they were used to would mean the Council having to find more money. There was only one way to do this – by increasing the amount of **council tax** people had to pay.

What made it even more difficult for the Labour councillors was that they had only a small majority on the council over their rivals, the Liberal Democrats – a majority of two.

Local elections were coming up in May. If there was just a small swing towards the Liberal Democrats, then Labour would lose control of the Council.

A decision had to be taken about spending more on public services – and it had to be taken quickly.

They held a referendum in which people simply voted on whether to increase council tax or keep it at the old rate. Voters were warned that if they voted against a tax rise there would almost certainly have to be cuts in the education service.

Out of the 278,000 electors in Bristol, 40 per cent voted in the referendum. Of these, 54 per cent voted against an increase in council tax.

Teachers were furious at the result and threatened to go on strike if any teacher lost their job. They pointed out that about one in five secondary students in Bristol go to private schools and don't therefore use the Council education service. They also said that some people in Bristol send their children to school in neighbouring authorities.

? question

1. Bristol City Council needed to decide two things. Firstly, whether to spend more money on education, and secondly, if they decided to do this, how the extra cash would be raised.

   What are the different ways in which they can make these decisions?

■ What the Council did

Instead of deciding the issue themselves, the Labour councillors chose to let the people of Bristol decide.

? question

2. Do you think the Council's decision to hold a referendum was a wise one? Give reasons for your answer.

Democracy

What does it mean?

The decision on whether to increase council tax in Bristol was taken through a process of democracy.

This is a system of government where decisions are taken either by people directly or through representatives they have elected.

There are two types of democracy. *Direct* democracy is when people make their decisions together as a single group. *Representative* democracy is when people elect representatives to take decisions on their behalf, e.g. a local councillor, an MP or a school councillor.

Representative democracy, as we practise it today, contains a number of further characteristics. It is a form of government that:

- reflects and responds to public opinion
- has regular and free elections
- allows people to criticise what it does
- protects the rights of individuals and minority groups.

 questions

3. Which of the following issues do you think would be best decided by representative democracy and which by direct democracy? Why?

    a) whether to adopt the Euro as our currency
    b) whether the country should go to war
    c) whether we should have more religious or faith schools
    d) whether to ban smoking in all public places.

4. What do you think are the advantages and disadvantages of each of these different types of democracy?

Referendum

A referendum is the process of putting a specific political issue to the people as a whole, rather than their elected representatives.

In 1975 there was a referendum of the British people asking if they agreed with Britain's continued membership of the European Community. In 1998, the people of Wales were asked if they wanted a separate assembly.

Some would like to have more referendums because they feel that they give people more of a say in decisions that affect them. Others disagree, believing that some issues are too complex to be reduced to one or two simple questions and that referendums can work to the disadvantage of minority groups.

question

5. Are there any issues in Britain on which you think we ought to have a referendum? Explain your reasoning.

keywords

Council tax
A tax paid to the council by most householders based on the value of their property.

Local elections
Elections to choose councillors for the local council.

Public services
Services needed by the community as a whole, e.g. street lighting, education, waste disposal.

Voting and elections

The right to vote

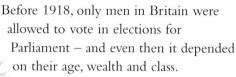

Before 1918, only men in Britain were allowed to vote in elections for Parliament – and even then it depended on their age, wealth and class.

In 1918, the vote was extended to all men aged 21 and over, and to women of 30 and over. In 1928 the voting age for women was lowered to 21 and they were, for the first time, in the same position as men. The present voting age of 18 was set in 1969.

■ Low turnout

The number of people turning out to vote in **general elections** in this country has been going down for several years. In 1997, 71 per cent of those eligible voted. In 2001, this fell to 59 per cent.

Natalie's story 'I did not vote in the last election. Do you want to know why?

'Imagine this. There are two blokes who fancy me. I'm not that impressed by either, but I am beginning to think I shall never ever meet anyone nice. If I was forced, I suppose I would say that one of them is not quite as bad as the other. My best friend said she thought he was "really quite nice". But my heart's not in it – even the thought of going out with him makes me feel slightly sick. So I decide to ignore them both and hold out for someone better.

'That's why I didn't vote in the last election. It wasn't because I had better things to do, or it was raining, or I think politicians are all alike or just because I couldn't be bothered. It was because there wasn't any party that really reflected my views.'

? questions

1. What was Natalie's reason for not voting? Was it a good reason?

2. Is it important if people don't vote in elections? What are your views?

3. Some people would say that Natalie was wrong for not voting. Here are some arguments they might use. Which do you think are the strongest, and why?

No respect It is disrespectful to those who fought and died in two world wars not to protect the rights we have today.

No control By opting out she is letting politicians do what they like.

No say She is throwing away her chance to have a say in the way the country is run.

Responsibility She has a responsibility to vote as a citizen.

Sets a bad example Where would this country be if nobody voted at all?

Struggle She should remember the struggle that women had to get the right to vote.

■ Reasons

After the low turnout in the 2001 general election, researchers tried to find out why fewer people had voted.

It was discovered that the largest drop in voting was among those in the 18–24

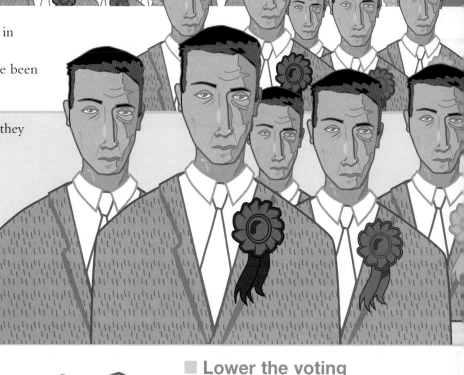

age range, with 20 per cent fewer voting than in 1997.

Several explanations for the low turnout have been put forward:

Contentment People didn't vote because they were happy with the way things were.

All the same Many saw little difference between one political party and another.

Foregone conclusion Many thought that the Labour Party would almost certainly win the election (which it did) therefore there was little point in voting.

Irrelevant Some didn't vote because they felt that politics didn't affect them.

What can be done?

Here are some suggestions to increase the numbers who turn out to vote at elections.

Easy vote Let people vote from home by phone or the Internet – or in their local supermarket.

Education Teach more about politics at school.

Incentives Allow people who vote to pay less in tax, say £10, or make voting compulsory, as they do in Australia.

Presentation The political parties should do more to interest voters and make clearer exactly what they stand for.

Real people Make a big effort to make politicians more like ordinary people. Try to increase the number of female, black and Asian candidates.

VOTER CARD

Please return this card to the Election Official after voting.

SEQUOIA

Lower the voting age to 16

Some people argue that it is time to lower the voting age to 16. They say that if young people get married at 16 and work and pay taxes, they are old enough to vote.

Others disagree, believing that young people wouldn't understand enough about politics to use their vote wisely.

? question

4. What is your opinion of the proposals to increase turnout at elections? Are there any that you particularly favour? Why? Have you any suggestions of your own?

⬧ keyword

General election
An election to choose the MPs who will form a new parliament, held every five years or less.

Voting and elections

Election to Parliament

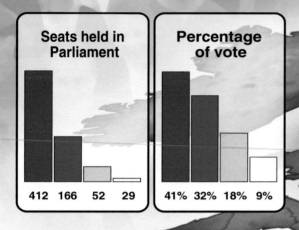

Seats held in Parliament: 412 166 52 29

Percentage of vote: 41% 32% 18% 9%

Labour
Conservative
Liberal Democrat
Other

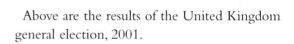

Constituencies

There are 659 MPs in Parliament, representing the whole of the United Kingdom – that is England, Northern Ireland, Scotland and Wales.

Almost all MPs represent a registered political party and each represents a defined area, called a constituency.

Elections

If an MP dies or resigns, a by-election is called to allow people to elect a new MP for their constituency.

At least every five years, a nationwide election must take place. This is known as a general election and voters in every constituency have the chance to re-elect or change their MP.

At the end of the general election, the party with the greatest number of MPs forms the new government, with the party leader becoming Prime Minister.

Voting

First-past-the-post Votes for general and by-elections in the United Kingdom are counted on a 'first-past-the-post' system. People each cast one vote and the winning candidate is the one with the most votes.

Above are the results of the United Kingdom general election, 2001.

? questions

1. Which party won the election in 2001?

2. If the 659 seats in Parliament had been allocated according to the percentage of the vote that each party had gained, how many seats would the Conservative, Labour and Liberal Democrat parties have each obtained? Can you see any criticisms that might be made against the first-post-the-post system?

Other voting systems

In recent years people in Britain have had the opportunity to vote for their representatives in the European Parliament, the National Assembly for Wales, the Scottish Parliament, the London Assembly, and the Northern Ireland Assembly.

CANDIDATE	PARTY	YO OR CL
EVANS, Annabel	Labour	
FERGUSON, Robert	Conservative	
KINGSLEY, Mica	Liberal Democrat	
JONES, Martin	Plaid Cymru	
RAMIREZ, Joseph	Green Party	
SAMPSON, Emma	Independent Socia	

The process of counting the votes is complicated because it uses (or transfers) people's second, third and fourth choices, etc, to decide who are the most popular candidates overall.

In a constituency where four seats are available, the four candidates who come top of the poll become the local representatives. People who favour this system argue that it allows voters the most choice and gives a fair reflection of the popularity of each party.

None of these has used the first-past-the-post system described above.

Instead, other systems have been used, designed to produce a more representative result. Three of these systems are described below.

List system In the election of Members of the European Parliament in 1999, voters cast one vote – not for individuals, but for a party. When the votes were added up, each party got the number of seats equal to the share of their vote. In this way a party that won 20 per cent of the vote was awarded 20 per cent of the seats.

Additional member system Everyone voting under this system has two votes. The first is cast for the *person* they want to be their constituency representative. The winner in each constituency is simply the person who gets the most votes.

The second is used to vote for their favourite *party*. After all these votes have been counted, further seats are awarded to additional representatives in such a way that the overall party representation in each area reflects that party's share of the vote. This system has been used in the elections for the Assemblies for Wales and for London, and also for the Scottish Parliament.

Single transferable vote This system is complicated for election officials to count, but very simple for the voter to use.

Each ballot paper indicates the number of seats available in the constituency and the names of all those standing for election. All the voter has to do is to number the candidates in order of preference.

? questions

3. You can test the different ways of voting for yourself through a mini-election in your classroom.

   • **Step 1** Select a number of candidates from the class. Choose at least one for each of the three main parties, but ideally include one or two minority parties, such as the Green Party.

   • **Step 2** Make sure everyone has: a list of the candidates; an outline of their policies; a ballot paper.

   • **Step 3** Everyone puts a *1* against the candidate of their first choice, and a *2* against the candidate of their second choice.

   • **Step 4** Collect in the ballot papers and count the first choice votes. This produces the winning candidate (and party) by first-past-the-post.

   • **Step 5** Now add the second choice votes to the first choice ones, and work out the total number of votes for each candidate. This uses the system of the single transferable vote.

4. Compare your results using the two systems. What do you notice?

Party politics

This unit looks at political parties and asks what influence the mass media has on our political views.

Join the party

Imagine

When Channel 4 conducted a poll of the British public to find the all time top 100 British Number 1 singles, first place went to John Lennon's *Imagine*.

The words of the song carry a political message – a vision of the way in which society could be run. Many people probably wouldn't want to live like this - imagine no possessions – but for some, the words of the song do say at least something about the kind of society that they would like to see.

Imagine no possessions,
I wonder if you can,
No need for greed or hunger,
A brotherhood of man,
Imagine all the people
Sharing all the world...

? questions

1. Imagine you had the opportunity to change three things that you believe would benefit society as a whole. What would they be? You might like to think about this at three levels – locally, nationally and internationally.

2. Select one of your suggestions and describe *how* it might be achieved.

Political views

Many of the answers you gave to Question 1 were probably similar to those of the others in your group. Most of us would like to see an end to war or poverty, or an improvement in the environment.

Where we tend to differ, however, is in deciding *how* these things might be achieved. Do we end fighting by heavy bombing? Do we help the poor by taxing the rich? Do we reduce pollution by building nuclear power stations?

Ideas into action

Protest Sometimes we become so concerned about a problem we take action ourselves. When a local school or hospital is threatened with closure, parents, children and teachers may protest either as individuals or as a group.

Pressure groups If the issue is of wider significance we might join or support a national or international group. The RSPCA and Oxfam are examples of these. Campaigning organisations of this kind are known as pressure groups.

Political parties Political parties are organisations interested in a much wider range of issues than pressure groups. They also tend to have certain principles or ideas that run through many of their policies and have the overall aim of governing the country.

The Conservative Party has its roots in the landowning and business classes of the eighteenth and nineteenth centuries. It has traditionally stood for free enterprise – the right of people to make the most of their talents – and opposes excessive interference by government. It traditionally supports the monarchy and sees Britain playing an important and independent role on the world's stage.

The Labour Party was jointly formed in 1906 by the trades unions and a left-wing political group called the Fabian Society. It has almost always been associated with ways of improving the situation of working people, for example through council housing and the National Health Service, which it introduced in 1945. Until recently, the party has also believed that key industries – like coal and rail – were so important that they should be run by the state.

The Liberal Democrat Party emphasises the need to protect individual rights and freedoms, particularly from abuse by the State, and supports close links with the remainder of Europe. The party has proposed higher taxes to pay for public services like education and health and has also pressed for many years for a change in the current voting system, which it regards as unfair.

Other parties in England and Wales include *Plaid Cymru*, which aims to secure self-government for Wales; and the *Green Party*, which seeks to change the way we live to produce a fairer society and one that ceases to damage the ecology of our planet.

? questions

3. Try to find out these parties' policies on a number of issues. You could choose from a list that includes crime, education, environment, taxation, transport etc.

4. It is sometimes said that there is little difference between the main political parties. What does your research (above) show about this?

British National Party supporters

Tolerance?

The *British National Party (BNP)* puts out misleading information and ideas particularly about immigrants and refugees. It is very critical of black and white people mixing and integrating, and implies that the presence of immigrants and refugees in Britain is strongly linked to problems we have in health care, education and housing. The BNP calls for the voluntary resettlement of immigrants 'to their lands of ethnic origin'.

The law

Freedom of expression is allowed under the *Human Rights Act* but this may be limited to preserve public order and protect the rights of others. It is an offence to publish and to possess racially inflammatory material, unless it can be shown that there was no intention to stir up racial hatred.

? question

5. Should parties be allowed to campaign on policies like these? What are the arguments for and against banning such parties?

Party politics

Newspapers

■ Read all about it

On Monday 6 October 1998, just as the annual Conservative Party conference was getting under way, the headline in that morning's *Sun* read 'This party is no more...it has ceased to be...this is an ex-party.'

With William Hague's (the former Conservative Party leader) head attached to the body of a parrot pictured hanging upside down, the newspaper went on to say 'Like Monty Python's parrot, it has fallen off its perch.'

The newspaper was commenting on the damage that the Conservative Party was inflicting on itself with its very public arguments over how closely Britain should be tied to the rest of Europe.

How do articles like this affect the way in which people vote?

THIS PARTY IS NO MORE... IT HAS CEASED TO BE... THIS IS AN EX-PARTY.

☐ Party preference

Most national newspapers tend to favour one political party in particular – although this is not as rigid as it used to be.

Until the mid-1990s the *Daily Mirror*, the *Guardian*, and the *Independent* were the only national daily papers not to support the Conservatives. But, by the time of the 2001 general election, most newspapers were recommending that their readers should vote Labour. Only the *Daily Mail* and *Daily Telegraph* remained staunchly Conservative.

Bias
Newspapers also exert political influence through how and what they report.

Michael Foot, Labour Party leader in the early 1980s, is remembered by many people for what he wore, rather than for what he did. At a Remembrance Day service in London he was photographed wearing an old jacket, which some thought was not suitable for such an occasion. Those newspapers that were critical of the Labour Party at the time gave this picture great prominence, suggesting that a party whose leader dressed in this way was not fit for government.

We have already seen (page 82) how some newspapers have used words such as *wave*, *flood* and *tide* to describe the arrival of asylum seekers, deliberately raising readers' concerns.

Profit All newspapers, and much of television and radio, are businesses trying to make a profit for their shareholders. Six companies publish 80 per cent of our daily, Sunday and local newspapers. This means that a relatively small number of people have a major influence over what we read.

✳ coursework idea

Collect a number of articles that show how newspapers either try to influence the political opinion of their readers or to persuade the government to change its policies. Explain how the newspaper is trying to do this and identify the issue on which it is writing.

Radio and television

SO, GENTLEMEN, ARE YOU FOR OR AGAINST THE *EURO?*

■ Balance

Radio and television stations are under much tighter control than newspapers over the way they broadcast news and political information. By law, both state run (the BBC) and independent radio and television stations must present and report news in a fair and balanced way. But this does not prevent radio and television from being criticised at times for the way in which they report the news.

Unlike newspapers, radio and television stations must not tell their listeners and viewers whom to vote for in an election. In fact on the day of the poll, the only political news that may be broadcast is simply that an election is taking place. There is no discussion of policies, winners and losers, or even the numbers turning out to vote, until the election is over and polling stations have closed.

■ Public opinion

Newspapers, radio and television, and the political parties themselves regularly carry out surveys into which party people favour and how they intend to vote. Opinion polls can be an important way of measuring what voters think.

However, some people feel we should follow the example of France and ban opinion polls completely during the period of an election. They say that knowing that the Conservatives are well ahead of Labour (or vice versa) distorts the whole election process.

? questions

3. In 2002 the BBC asked people in Wales how they would vote in a referendum on the Euro. These were the results.

- 41 per cent said they would vote *Yes* to joining the common currency
- 40 per cent said they would vote *No*
- 15 per cent replied *Don't know*
- 4 per cent said they would not vote at all

a) How might a newspaper in favour of Britain joining the Euro present these figures?

b) How might they be presented by a newspaper that is against our membership of the Euro?

c) How would you interpret the figures in an accurate and balanced way?

? questions

1. What factors do you think determine how people vote? Draw up a list and decide what you think are the most significant.

2. What is your impression of the way in which political events are reported? When people vote, do you think they really understand the political issues? Can you suggest any ways in which people can be better informed?

Campaigning

This unit shows how community action can be used to bring about change and asks what people need to do to improve their chances of success.

Home alone

Florence Okolo arrived in Britain from Nigeria to join her husband, who was a student in Manchester. Florence brought with her their two daughters, Awele and Anwuli. A year later, she gave birth to their third child, a baby boy.

The family had been together in Britain for two years when Florence and her husband separated. Florence's husband went back to Nigeria, taking his small son with him.

Florence stayed in Manchester with her daughters. She had a home, a job and she belonged to the local church. The girls attended primary school, and the whole family felt that they had become part of the community.

However, when her husband returned to Nigeria, Florence and her family ceased to have any legal right to remain in Britain as they did not have British citizenship. It took some time for this to come to the notice of the authorities – but four years after arriving here, Florence received a letter from the **Home Office** ordering her, Awele and Anwuli to leave.

Florence did not want to return to Nigeria. She decided to do as much as she could to ensure that she and her daughters stayed in Britain.

? question

1. Florence had to persuade the Home Office that she and Awele and Anwuli should not be deported. This would be difficult to do alone, as she had no family in Britain and relatively little money.

   What do you think Florence could do? Who could she find to help her with her case?

■ Help

Florence went to a solicitor who specialised in immigration cases of this kind. He agreed to take up her case, but also suggested that she should ask for help from Awele and Anwuli's school.

As soon as he heard about the problem, the head-teacher, Mr Dalby, said he would do as much as he possibly could. He told the teachers and school governors and explained the situation to the whole school.

The problem that they all faced is what to do. How do you mount a campaign to stop someone from being deported when you have never done anything like that before?

? question

2. How could the school show support for the girls? Who should they try to influence? Who can help them? What should they do?

■ Tactics

Over the next four years Florence, her lawyer, the school and the church did as much as they could to make sure that Florence and her family stayed in Britain. This is what they did.

• *Putting the case* The lawyer prepared the documents that set out why Florence should be given special permission to remain in Britain. He made sure they were filled in correctly, presented on time, and clearly set out to show why it would be unfair to require Florence and her family to leave Britain.

When Florence's application to stay in Britain was turned down, her lawyer prepared the papers for an appeal to the Home Secretary. Again he had to make out the best possible case on Florence's behalf.

• *Support* Letters, asking for help, were written to Florence's local MP and the city council in Manchester. The MP, the mayor and the city council all gave Florence their support.

• *Publicity* Florence and her supporters needed to get members of the general public to support her case.

They wrote letters, made posters and talked to the media. They organised marches and demonstrations and always tried to make sure that the newspapers, radio or television covered them.

They held rallies in Manchester outside the city hall and in one of the parks, and also took their case

to London – with demonstrations outside the Houses of Parliament and the Royal Courts of Justice. They didn't just involve adults, but children too, particularly those from Awele and Anwuli's school.

■ Success

The Home Office at first turned down Florence's application to stay in Britain, but did allow her to submit an appeal. This too was rejected. With few chances remaining, her supporters were able to arrange for her to meet the Home Secretary, with her solicitor, to put her case in person. A month after this meeting, Florence received a letter giving her permission to stay in Britain.

? questions

3. What do you think were the three most important reasons why Florence's campaign succeeded?

4. Who benefited from the campaign? Explain why.

❖ keyword

Home Office
A government department with responsibilities that include law and order and immigration. The Home Secretary is the head of the Home Office.

Campaigning

We want our bus back!

Bus stop

The notice in the paper read 'As from 1 March the 7.55 a.m. service to Bedford will be withdrawn.'

'It is so annoying,' said Lena to her mum. 'We rely on that service to get us to school. If they take it off, we'll have to leave home at five past seven.'

'You could find out why they are doing it,' said her mum, 'and a letter of complaint wouldn't do any harm either.'

The following day Lena asked the bus driver why they were taking the service off. 'Not enough passengers,' said the driver. 'If they put it on half-an-hour later at 8.25, they can almost fill this bus with people going into town for shopping and work.'

 question

1. The next morning Lena asked some of her friends on the bus if they could do anything together to save the service. Here are some of the answers she received.

   - 'It's not our responsibility.'

   - 'No one will listen to us, we're just kids.'

   - 'We won't go to school.'

   - 'It's up to the bus company what it wants to do.'

   - 'We should get teachers or parents to do something about it.'

   - 'It's too complicated.'

   Do you agree with these comments? Write down what you would say in reply.

Starting off

Lena and two of her friends decided that they would write to complain. The next day they sent a letter to the bus company asking why the 7.55 bus was being discontinued and explaining how much they relied on the service.

A week later they received a reply saying that not enough people used the service and that it was therefore uneconomic. Although the company regretted the inconvenience, the service would still be changed in just under two months, as planned.

? question

2. If they are to continue with their campaign, what can Lena and her friends do next? Draw up a list of ideas, and then select those that you think would be the most effective.

Action

The three friends decided to organise a petition, collecting signatures from everyone who used the bus. They took some photographs of this and sent the pictures to the local newspaper and the petition to the bus company. They also made posters for display in local shops.

CHILDREN'S PETITION to save bus

? questions

3. What tactics did the students use in their campaign?

4. What do you think were the most significant things that brought them success?

5. What issues are people campaigning about in your area? Are they national or local problems? What tactics do they use to put forward their cause?

'We also thought it would be a good idea to ask the school for help,' said Lena. 'After all, that's why we need the bus.'

The head suggested that Lena wrote to the county council, which has the power to keep important loss-making services going. She added that she and the school governors would also write a letter supporting Lena's case.

'We arranged a meeting with our local county councillor, and wrote to our MP. We also kept the paper informed about our campaign,' said Lena. 'We met the reporter several times and always tried to find a way of getting a photograph in as well. Twice we made it onto the front page.

'Eventually we managed to persuade the county council to talk to the bus operator about ways of getting the service put back on. The council has some money that they can use to subsidise a service if they feel it is worthwhile. Finally they reached an agreement, and six weeks after our campaign began, the bus company decided not to cut the 7.55.'

Pressure groups

Groups of people campaigning for change or trying to influence government policy are known as pressure groups. They can be local and very small, like Lena and her friends; or they can much larger with international connections. Greenpeace and Amnesty International are examples of these.

Sometimes they work quietly behind the scenes, trying to influence important decisions. On other occasions they seek maximum publicity with big campaigns.

? questions

6. What are the differences and similarities between pressure groups and political parties?

7. More people belong to pressure groups than to political parties. Can you explain why?

✳ coursework idea

Find out something about a pressure group of your choice. Most national and international groups have their own website.

What is the main issue about which they campaign? Who are they trying to influence? How do they do this? How do they get the money for all their activities?

Do you support the aims of the group and would you consider joining them? Explain your thinking.

Big world, small world?

This unit examines some of the benefits and drawbacks of globalisation.

Globalisation

Long haul

In 1994 one of the longest trials in British history began when McDonald's Corporation sued two protestors, Helen Steel and David Morris, over the contents of a leaflet that they and others had distributed on behalf of London Greenpeace.

The leaflet, entitled *What's wrong with McDonald's?*, strongly criticised the food that McDonald's sold and many of the ways in which the company operated. McDonald's hotly disputed these accusations, and asked those responsible to withdraw their comments. Some agreed, but Helen Steel and David Morris did not, and legal action followed.

It took almost *three years* for both sides to deliver their evidence. McDonald's used a large team of lawyers to present their case. Helen Steel and David Morris conducted their own defence. The judge decided that most of the serious allegations made against the company were untrue, and awarded McDonald's £110,000 damages, later reduced on appeal to £40,000.

Worldwide scale

One point raised in the leaflet was the scale of the McDonald's operations. The McDonald's Corporation has more than 28,000 restaurants in 120 countries. McDonald's is not alone in this. Many companies have a worldwide presence, and their products are household names.

Companies operating in a number of different countries are called *multinationals* and are a reflection and a part of the process of *globalisation*.

Globalisation refers to the process in which business, politics and culture operate on a world stage, no longer confined to single countries or continents.

The term was originally coined in the 1980s, but the idea itself goes back more than five hundred years.

The long view Between the fifteenth and nineteenth centuries, Britain, and several other European nations, colonised many parts of the world – in effect, trying to spread their rule and influence across the globe. In doing this, they exported their languages and their religions, and set up governments and administrations that often exactly mirrored the arrangements that they had at home.

Local people were used as cheap labour and were often forcibly moved from one area to another. This was the basis of slavery, where millions of Africans were shipped to work in the Caribbean and America.

The colonisers also amassed huge amounts of wealth from their overseas colonies. Food, plants and other raw materials that had previously been restricted to certain parts of Africa, Asia or the Americas, arrived for the first time in Europe. Fruits, spices, coffee, tea and certain types of timber and fur became known for the first time on a *global* scale, no longer restricted to their region or country of origin.

■ The situation today

The process of globalisation is believed to have accelerated and developed over the last 25 to 30 years. It has also changed its nature. There are several reasons for this.

> WITH ACCESS TO A COMPUTER, THE **COST** OF SENDING AN E-MAIL ANYWHERE IN THE WORLD IS VIRTUALLY **NIL**.

• *Communications* Technological developments in phones, faxes and computers have made communications throughout the world simpler, faster and cheaper.

• *Transport* Lower costs and improved technology have led to a massive increase in the movement of people and goods around the world.

> AIRLINE TICKETS ARE NOW SOMETIMES **CHEAPER** THAN RAIL FARES.

• *Politics and economics* The 1980s and 1990s were a period of great political and economic change. The Soviet Union was dismantled into separate independent states. There was also a big reduction in the role of the state in the USA and Europe (particularly in Britain, under the influence of Mrs Thatcher). Companies became much freer to move their operations to different parts of the world and to invest capital overseas.

> IN BRITAIN AND ELSEWHERE A NUMBER OF **STATE-OWNED** ENTERPRISES INCLUDING TELEPHONE, GAS, ELECTRICITY, WATER, RAILWAYS, AND THE NATIONAL AIRLINE WERE SOLD TO BECOME **PRIVATE BUSINESSES**.

Size matters There are ASDA supermarkets in many British towns and cities. The company was formed in 1965 by a group of farmers from Yorkshire. In 1999 it was taken over by Wal-Mart, an American corporation with stores throughout the United States – and in 2001, Wal-Mart recorded the largest sales of any company in the *world*.

The figures below give an indication of how large some businesses have become. The examples – a supermarket, two car makers, and a company whose products include beer, cigarettes and many different brands of food – show companies with sales in excess of the value of all the goods and services (GDP) produced in some *countries*.

2001 Turnover

Wal-Mart Stores	General Motors	Ford Motor Co.	Philip Morris
$219 billion	$177 billion	$162 billion	$72 billion

2001 GDP

Belgium	Turkey	Denmark	Pakistan
$226 billion	$199 billion	$162 billion	$61 billion

✳ coursework idea

Find one or more reports from the media about some aspect of globalisation. Using the Internet you will be able to obtain an overseas perspective. Explain the issue and compare how the story is reported in the different sources. What is your view of the problem and the measures that should or should not be taken?

Big world, small world

Anti-globalisation

DEFEND OUR FORESTS CLEARCUT THE WTO

■ Protest

In November 1999, an estimated 100,000 demonstrators marched through the streets of Seattle on the west coast of the United States, where members of the World Bank were meeting.

The protest was the first of many that have since taken place in other cities throughout the world – including Berlin, London, Moscow and Prague.

The protestors at Seattle and elsewhere tend to be a mixture of people – trade unionists, environmentalists, students and workers – mostly sharing the belief that globalisation does more harm than good.

While the majority try to protest peacefully, many of the demonstrations have resulted in violence, with damage to buildings and shops and running battles with the police. In the Italian city of Genoa in 2001 a protestor was killed as he attacked the police.

Targets Large-scale anti-globalisation protests have tended to be held at meetings of the World Trade Organisation, the International Monetary Fund and the World Bank. These are organisations of countries that promote trade and provide loans to help countries in crisis.

The protestors believe that the rules governing world trade tend to meet the interests of large business corporations, rather than the needs of ordinary people.

Criticism 'Cheap sloganeering and mindless vandalism' was the description of the protests given by one person interviewed by the BBC after demonstrations in 2001 at Davos in Switzerland.

Others critics are more thoughtful. They agree that some protestors attend largely to stir up trouble and that many probably don't understand all the issues involved. 'But at least they are doing something,' they say. 'How else can you change things when many of the people with power are accountable to no one but their **shareholders**. If we don't like our politicians we can vote them out of office. How do we get these people to listen to us?'

? question

1. How should people protest or make their opinions known over issues of this kind? What do you think are the limits to acceptable protest?

The case for globalisation...

Japanese companies set up electronics factories and car manufacturing plants in Britain. A joint British-Dutch company produces and sells ice cream in China. Kenyan farmers send flowers and vegetables to Europe. These are some of the things taking place in the global market. Those in favour of these trends see them as the best chance of improving standards of living in the world as a whole.

Governments generally see multinationals as a force for good. They create work, spread wealth, introduce new technology and help people learn better ways of doing business. Many companies also work for the good of the local community, with projects to improve education, health and the environment.

Globalisation gives millions of people choices and access to goods and services. It increases wealth, enhances human liberty and helps us better understand our neighbours.

... and the case against

Opponents of globalisation are worried about the level of influence that large corporations and multinational companies have in the world today.

Although governments usually welcome foreign investment in their country, opponents state that the benefits of this can be short-lived. Promises of employment sometimes mean that measures to protect the environment are ignored. Critics also say that there is nothing to stop the foreign investor pulling out if better opportunities for profits appear elsewhere, leaving many workers without jobs.

Too many foreign imports damage a country's industry and culture. Giant companies, they say, squeeze out traditional local producers and limit choice.

Many multinationals set up plants or operations in less developed countries in order to take advantage of cheaper labour or a plentiful supply of raw materials. Some companies are criticised for offering much poorer pay and working conditions to workers overseas than they do to those at home.

? question

2. Which of the following statements do you most agree with? Explain why.

a) Globalisation is a force for good and should be encouraged.
b) Generally the advantages of globalisation outweigh the drawbacks.
c) Greater controls should be placed on large companies to make sure that they work for the benefit of the community and not just their investors.
d) Globalisation should be opposed at all costs.

coursework ideas

• Many companies run community programmes. Details will be provided on their website or in their annual report, available in large libraries. You may wish to undertake a small study of one of these, outlining the nature of the programme and critically assessing the benefits and possible drawbacks.

• Community programmes can also provide opportunities for you or your school to become involved in activities locally, nationally or overseas.

keywords

Shareholder
Someone who invests in a company.

Big world, small world

Trade

■ The end of the line

After more than a century of manufacture, the Raleigh factory in Nottingham closed in 2002, and production of one of the most famous makes of bicycle moved to China. With much lower labour rates, and good production techniques, cycles can be produced in China for 25 per cent less than in Britain.

Raleigh's decision to assemble their products elsewhere is not unusual. A glance at the labels on many of the goods that we buy shows how common it is for companies to set up overseas operations.

Small steps A 2002 Oxfam study of factories in Indonesia, employing workers to make Nike and Adidas shoes, found that some improvements had been made in recent years, but its conclusion still makes grim reading.

? question

1. What are the likely consequences of a firm moving its manufacturing base overseas? Who tends to benefit and who tends to lose?

■ Terms and conditions

One significant effect of building a factory overseas is the new work that it brings to that area. This can be a great benefit – but it raises the question of exactly how that factory should be run. What levels of pay and working conditions should Raleigh adopt for their new factory overseas? Is it acceptable if they are lower than those of their remaining employees in Britain?

Fair game? Since the late 1980s there has been much criticism of the conditions of workers in less developed countries who are employed to make clothing and equipment for a number of large multinational corporations in the sports and leisure industries.

Companies such as Nike and Adidas have been among those singled out for criticism over the excessive working hours and low pay endured by those who make their goods.

Oxfam

• *Wages* With full-time wages as low as \$US2 (£1.30), workers live in extreme poverty and those with children must either send them to distant villages to be looked after by relatives or else go into debt to meet their basic needs.

Oxfam

• *Working conditions* Workers report that although there has been some reduction in the physical and psychological pressures under which they work, they continue to be shouted at and humiliated and to work in dangerous conditions.

Oxfam

• *Unions* Workers have reason to fear that active union involvement could lead them to be dismissed, jailed or physically assaulted.

■ Power and profit

One reason why Nike and Adidas have been criticised so heavily is because they are powerful multinational companies making large profits through their sales. Together they control almost half the US athletic footwear market. Nike's net income for 2000/2001 was $589m (about £390m). In 2001, the *Los Angeles Times* reported that the company was paying Tiger Woods $100m over a five-year period to endorse their products.

■ Fair shares

Almost all manufactured goods go through several stages before they reach the customer. At each one, the worker, the factory owner and the retailer will need to be paid. But how much should they get?

? question

2. Trainers vary greatly in price. Imagine a pair on sale in a sports shop in Britain for £50. The four major groups involved in getting them to the stores are: the factory *worker*, the factory *owner*, the owner of the *brand*, and the *retailer*.

   What would be a *fair* way of splitting the £50 sale price between each of these? Explain your thinking.

   How much would you estimate *in reality* is received by each of these four groups? What is your comment on this?

■ Taking action

A quarter of the people on this planet live in poverty. There are 1.2 billion people who live on less than 65p per day.

In the mid 1990s, the governments of many countries, including Britain, agreed to try to cut world poverty by half by the year 2015. This involves many different kinds of support, including aid, training, making it easier for less developed countries to sell their goods, and removing the debt of poorer nations.

In 1972, Britain signed an agreement under which industrialised countries would give 0.7 per cent of their GNP (gross national product) in overseas aid. In 2001, Britain's figure was 0.36 per cent. Although below the target, it was greater than that of a number of other industrialised countries including France, Germany, Japan and the US.

? question

3. Do countries with a higher than average standard of living have a responsibility to give aid to those who do not? Explain your views.

Global warming

This unit asks what action should be taken in view of what we know about changes in world climate.

The problem

■ Breakaway

The Antarctic ice sheet is the largest body of ice on the planet. At its thickest, it is more than 4.5 km deep and holds 90 per cent of the earth's fresh water.

The amount of ice contained in the sheet fluctuates, with more in winter than in summer. It is quite normal for small parts of the ice sheet to break off – these form icebergs, which gradually melt as they drift north.

Scientists have known for many years that ice caps over both the North and South Poles are melting. However, in early 2002, two exceptionally large pieces of ice broke off the Antarctic ice sheet – one with an area of more than three thousand square km – roughly the size of Norfolk.

For those scientists who studied the climate of the world this was a very significant sign of global warming.

■ Evidence

Temperatures throughout the world are gradually rising, with a significant increase recorded over the last 25 years. Temperatures in the 1990s were the warmest on record. Scientists identified a further rise in world temperatures early in 2002.

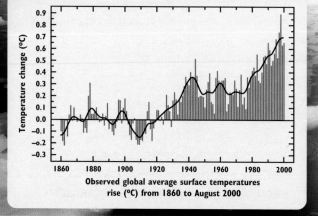
Observed global average surface temperatures rise (°C) from 1860 to August 2000

? question

1. **Look at the graph below showing changes in global temperature between 1860 and 2000. Make at least two observations about the information shown.**

■ Explanation

Climate change over long periods of time is quite normal. There is evidence that a mini ice age began in Europe about 500 years ago and pictures painted of the River Thames in the early 1700s suggest that winters then were probably much colder than they are now.

However, scientists now almost universally agree that the changes that we have experienced since the 1980s are *not* part of this 'natural' variation in climate, but are caused by the burning of fossil fuels.

 **The greenhouse effect** The atmosphere of the earth is warmed by energy from the sun. Much of this heat is reflected back into space, but some is trapped inside a layer of gases that surround the earth. This is called the greenhouse effect and stops the earth from cooling down too quickly. Without it, temperatures on earth would be 30° centigrade lower.

The layer of gas surrounding the earth is made up of water vapour, methane, nitrous oxide and carbon dioxide, all of which occur quite naturally as part of the cycle of life on earth.

However, the burning of fossil fuels over the last 200 years for power, manufacturing and transport is believed by most scientists to have changed the composition of this insulating blanket. Raising the level of greenhouse gases in the atmosphere has trapped energy from the sun that would otherwise escape – creating what we know as global warming.

Consequences

Scientists cannot predict exactly how the climate in specific parts of the world will change. But there is a general belief that the number of hot summer days in Europe, North America and parts of South America will increase and the number of exceptionally cold days will decline.

It is also predicted that higher overall temperatures will produce an increase in extreme weather conditions, such as high winds, floods and droughts.

The floods that affected many parts of Britain in 2000 were frequently linked in the news with global warming. But not all scientists agreed with this. The head of the meteorological service in Britain said that although global warming could have caused the severe storms, they were not in themselves actually proof that it was taking place.

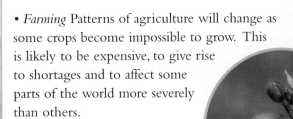

Predictions

• *Sea levels* The melting of glaciers and ice caps could, by the end of the twenty-first century, cause sea levels to rise by between 15 and 90 cm. This would put a number of places at risk. Low-lying parts of Bangladesh would be flooded, as would parts of major coastal cities such as London, New York and Bangkok.

• *Farming* Patterns of agriculture will change as some crops become impossible to grow. This is likely to be expensive, to give rise to shortages and to affect some parts of the world more severely than others.

• *Flora and fauna* Some species of animals and plants will disappear, unable to adapt to changing climatic conditions.

• *Natural disasters* Forecasters predict an increase in natural disasters such as flooding, drought, disease and forest fires. All areas would be vulnerable, but experience suggests that disasters would occur more often in developing countries, where there are fewer ways of combating them.

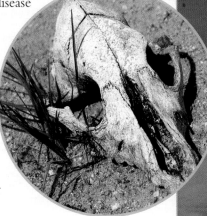

? question

2. A very basic question facing governments today is whether they should take any steps to reduce global warming. What are the arguments in favour of taking action now? What are the arguments against? What would you recommend?

Global warming

The solution

■ Who's who?

There are 210 countries in the world. The tables below show the ten with the highest carbon dioxide emissions, and the ten with the lowest.

The highest ...

▦	USA	1 480 000 000 tons
	China	840 000 000 tons
	Russia	390 000 000 tons
●	Japan	300 000 000 tons
	India	280 000 000 tons
	Germany	220 000 000 tons
▨	United Kingdom	140 000 000 tons
	Canada	120 000 000 tons
	Italy	110 000 000 tons
	Mexico	100 000 000 tons

... and the lowest

	Uganda	20 000 000 tons
	Cambodia	20 000 000 tons
	Zaire	10 000 000 tons
	Afghanistan	10 000 000 tons
	Mali	10 000 000 tons
	Burundi	10 000 000 tons
	Ethiopia	10 000 000 tons
	Chad	less than 10 000 000 tons
	Namibia	less than 10 000 000 tons
	Turks & Caicos Islands	less than 10 000 000 tons

CO2 emissions, 1998. Source: Oak Ridge National Laboratory and the University of North Dakota

■ questions

1. What observations can you make about the figures shown in the tables opposite?

2. Leaders at the Earth Summit needed to decide how to reduce carbon dioxide emissions worldwide. Here are some of their options.

   A Let every country decide for itself by how much to reduce its emissions.

   B Agree that every country should cut their emissions by a fixed percentage e.g. 10 per cent, before a certain date.

   C Require the more prosperous industrialised countries, like the United States, Japan, Britain and Germany, to reduce their emission levels before those of poorer, non-industrial countries.

   What are the strengths and weakness of each choice? Which one would you propose, and why?

■ Warning

The first person to use the phrase *greenhouse effect* was the French mathematician Jean Baptiste Fourier in 1827. In 1938 a British meteorologist, G.S. Callender, gathered information from 200 weather stations around the world and found a rise in world temperatures over the previous 50 years.

However, it took until the late 1970s before the nations of the world began to discuss global warming in any detail, with one of the first significant steps being taken at the Earth Summit, held in Rio de Janeiro in Brazil, in 1992.

■ Progress

The conference in Rio produced a number of important international agreements. One was to manage the environment in a way that met present needs without damaging our ability to meet those of the future. This idea is called *sustainable development* and part of the programme of action to achieve this is called **Agenda 21**.

A second agreement reached at the Rio Summit was to reduce levels of carbon dioxide – with industrial countries taking the lead, and developing countries following later.

Kyoto After a great deal of preparation and negotiation a point was reached in 1997 when most industrial countries were ready to sign a legally binding agreement promising to reduce their carbon emissions by an agreed amount. The venue was the Japanese city of Kyoto.

At the end of the conference most industrial countries, including Britain and the United States, had agreed to reduce their emissions by between five and seven per cent of 1990 levels between 2008 and 2012.

Developing countries agreed that they too would reduce emission in due course.

The rate of reduction was much lower than scientists had recommended – but, nevertheless, many thought that the Kyoto agreement was a significant step.

■ Change

In March 2001, shortly after he became President of the United States, George W. Bush announced that the United States had withdrawn its support for the Kyoto agreement.

Explaining the reason for his decision, Mr Bush said that the agreement would harm the US economy and hurt American workers. It was unfair, he said, to expect industrialised countries to reduce their levels of greenhouse gases when developing countries were not expected to do so.

US opinion polls taken immediately after the President's announcement indicated that the majority of American people disagreed with his decision.

Later Mr Bush stated that he would be introducing tax incentives designed to encourage US manufacturers to reduce their carbon emissions.

The United States has five per cent of world's population and accounts for almost a quarter of the world's carbon dioxide.

? questions

3. Do you think Mr Bush was right to withdraw from the Kyoto agreement? Explain your reasoning.

4. After Mr Bush's announcement the countries that had signed the treaty had to decide what to do. They could:

a) keep to the terms of their agreement, without the United States

b) call another conference and try to renegotiate an agreement that would be acceptable to the United States

c) dissolve the agreement completely.

Which would you recommend, and why?

5. What measures do individual people take to reduce global warming or other environmental problems? How far do we each have a personal responsibility to do this? Can we be of any influence?

❖ keywords

Agenda 21
The name given to a plan of action, drawn up at the Rio conference, and signed by the government of almost every country in the world. Under this agreement government and local authorities must develop special policies for achieving sustainable development – informing and consulting local people throughout.

Criminal law

The first topic in this unit explains how magistrates' courts work. These are local courts that hear a very large proportion of all criminal cases heard in court.

Inside a magistrates' court

Press
Reports of a trial may be given in the local or national media. In some circumstances, however, the press are not allowed to reveal the names of children involved in a case in order to prevent them from being identified. Victims of serious sexual assault are also protected in this way.

Witness stand

Legal adviser
A qualified lawyer, who advises magistrates on the law and on legal procedure. Formerly known as the justices' clerk.

Probation service
Probation officers provide magistrates with reports on the social circumstances of offenders, used to help magistrates decide on an appropriate sentence.

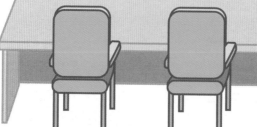

Public gallery

On trial

■ Criminal proceedings

Arrest The police have the power to arrest anyone they reasonably suspect of committing a crime. That person can be held for up to 24 hours, but must then normally be charged with an offence or cautioned or released.

Advice In almost all circumstances, anyone who is arrested or goes to a police station voluntarily is entitled to see a solicitor. This consultation is free and in private.

Charge If the police feel that they have enough evidence, they will charge the suspect with the offence.

The accused will then generally be released on bail and told when and where they are due to appear in court. If the offence is very serious, or the police have good reason to believe that the suspect will not attend court, they can apply to a magistrate to have the suspect held on remand in prison until the trial takes place.

Summons This is an order issued by a court requiring someone to appear in court on a certain date. This procedure is used only in less serious cases.

Crown Prosecution Service When the police have investigated an offence they pass the file to the Crown Prosecution Service who decides whether there is enough evidence for the case to proceed to court.

Magistrates' court All criminal cases are first brought to a magistrates' court – where most of them are dealt with. If the accused is aged 17 or under, the case will be heard in a youth court.

The more serious offences are passed on to the Crown Court if magistrates are satisfied that there is a reasonable case to be made out against the accused. In some cases, such as theft, defendants have the right to ask to be tried by a judge and jury, rather than magistrates. If the request is granted, these cases too are passed to the Crown Court

Crown Court A case in the Crown Court is heard by a judge, who presides over the trial and makes sure that it is run fairly. The verdict is reached by the jury and, if the defendant is found guilty, the judge will pass sentence.

Help with costs The accused is entitled to help with the cost of legal advice and the presentation of their case in court. This is funded by the Criminal Defence Service.

Magistrates

There are two kinds of magistrate, *lay justices* and *district judges*.

Lay justices are members of the local community, working as magistrates part-time, on average one day a fortnight, normally hearing cases in court in twos or threes. They are unpaid, except for expenses, and have no legal qualifications, but do receive training for their work as a magistrate. Lay justices are also known as *JPs*, or *justices of the peace*.

District judges do the same job as magistrates, but are trained and experienced lawyers and work in court alone.

Magistrates, clerks and solicitors wear ordinary clothes in court, and do not wear wigs.

Prosecution and defence

Lawyers for the prosecution and defence question each witness and each make opening and closing statements at the beginning and end of the trial.

If the accused has pleaded or been found guilty, the defence will probably suggest to the court why the defendant might be given a more lenient sentence – perhaps giving reasons why the defendant acted in a particular way or saying that the crime was totally out of character.

Defendant

Court usher

The usher escorts witnesses to and from the witness stand and helps with the smooth running of the court.

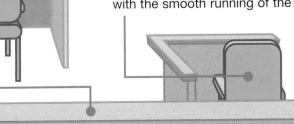

Criminal law

In court

■ The magistrate's tale

Michael Marks is a magistrate in Wolverhampton. Until he retired a year ago, he was a primary school head teacher.

'I sit in court for about 40 days a year. Last Friday I had two cases of shoplifting, a man accused of shooting his neighbour's cat, benefit fraud, and a serious assault, which went on to the Crown Court.

'I also sit on the youth bench, dealing with young offenders, trying to help them so they do not re-offend and again lead useful lives.

'I've lived in this area almost all my life – and I think the local knowledge that magistrates bring is invaluable.'

> ### ? questions
>
> 1. Most magistrates are a) local b) unpaid and c) have no legal training. Write down what you feel are the advantages and disadvantages of at least one of these points.

■ Drink driving

This is one of the cases that Michael Marks had to deal with.

The defendant Rhys Hughes, aged 34

The offence Driving a motor vehicle while over the prescribed alcohol limit, contrary to Section 5(1) of the Road Traffic Act 1988.

Plea Guilty

Prosecution evidence At 2.00 p.m., four days ago, the defendant drove his car into a stationary vehicle. No one was injured, but there was extensive damage to both cars. Following a positive breath test at the scene of the accident, the defendant was breathalysed again at the police station. This result was twice the legal level.

Defence statement Through his solicitor, Rhys Hughes explained that he had met his partner for lunch, and been told that she wished to end their three-year relationship. After his friend left, Rhys stayed in the restaurant and continued to drink. The accident occurred on his way back to work. Mr Hughes has worked for his employer for 16 years and believes he will lose his job if he is sent to prison.

Sentencing

• The defendant *must* be disqualified from driving for at least a year, and up to a maximum of three, unless there are special reasons not to do so.

• Magistrates *may* also impose one of the following, depending on how much the defendant is over the prescribed limit:

- a term of imprisonment for up to six months
- a fine of up to £5,000 (the average is £300–£400)
- a community penalty of up to 100 hours' community service
- require the defendant to attend a special course to help stop people from drinking and driving.

? questions

2. Is there anything else you need to know about Rhys Hughes before passing sentence? Why would this information be useful?

3. Look at the punishment tariff above and decide how you feel Rhys Hughes should be dealt with. Now draft Michael Mark's statement to the court announcing the magistrates' decision.

Local justice

Strong efforts are now made to try to make sure that magistrates reflect, as far as possible, the community in which they serve.

However, although there is now an equal balance of male and female magistrates, people from ethnic minorities are under-represented, as are those below the age of 40. In 2000, almost half the magistrates in England and Wales were retired and most came from professional or managerial backgrounds.

In court

Magistrates' duties

Magistrates handle more than 90 per cent of all criminal cases, but also deal with some civil cases. (You can check the difference between civil and criminal law on page 11.)

Civil law cases include matters of family law, such as the care of children and problems people face after the break-up of their family.

Other parts of a magistrate's caseload include the non-payment of council tax, granting licences for the sale of alcohol and deciding whether a person who has been arrested should be remanded in custody or allowed out on bail.

Youth courts

Specially trained magistrates also sit in youth courts, hearing cases involving young offenders, below the age of 18.

Powers

In criminal cases magistrates can impose a range of sentences, including fines of up to £5,000 and a sentence of up to six months' imprisonment, or two years' detention in a young offender institution for under 21s.

Qualifications

Magistrates must be between the ages of 27 and 65 when they are appointed and may continue to sit until they are 70. They must live close to the area served by the court to which they are appointed and must be of 'good character'.

? questions

4. What kind of person do you think would make a good magistrate? List the sort of qualities you think that person should have.

5. Why do you think people give up time to work unpaid as a magistrate?

6. What measures can you suggest that might ensure that magistrates are more representative of the communities that they serve?

Criminal law

Crown Court

This second topic looks at the working of the Crown Court – particularly from the viewpoint of the members of the jury.

Trial by jury

Tessa, 27, received a letter summoning her for jury service. Her name had been chosen by computer at random from the local electoral roll. She is instructed to report to the local Crown Court in six weeks' time. Jury service, it explains, will last a minimum of two weeks.

Tessa is not very keen to go. She works for a chain of hotels, and is very busy at the moment with conferences and all sorts of other things to organise. Having two weeks out will cause major problems.

She thinks it could be interesting to sit on a jury, but is worried about the thought of sending someone to prison.

Excuse me Government research shows that it is becoming increasingly difficult to obtain people to serve on a jury.

Two out of three who are summoned for jury service either put forward reasons why they shouldn't serve, or simply don't turn up. A significant number of these are well-educated people, working in business or the professions.

Ethnic minorities and younger people are also under-represented on juries, as their names are less likely to appear on the electoral roll.

? questions

1. What do you think Tessa should do? Does she have a responsibility to do jury service? Do you think pressure of work is a good reason for her to be excused?

2. Juries are supposed to reflect a cross-section of the general public. Does it matter if certain sections of the population are not represented?

3. Some people have argued that we should make it much harder for a person not to serve on a jury, with heavy penalties for those who fail to attend. What is your view?

4. Would you like to serve on a jury? Try to explain the reasons why, or why not. How would you respond to Tessa's point about her concern over sending someone to prison?

Crown Court

■ Juries

A jury sits in a Crown Court and has the job of deciding on the guilt or innocence of the accused, based on the evidence they hear in Court. A jury is made up of 12 adults, aged 18 to 70.

Ineligible Certain people may not serve on a jury. These mainly include those connected with the law, such as judges, magistrates, police officers, solicitors and prison officers, and also anyone who is on bail or has been on probation in the last five years or who has served a custodial sentence within the last ten years. Ministers of religion are also ineligible.

Excused Some people are *automatically* excused jury service if they wish. These include MPs, peers, people who work in the medical profession, members of the armed forces and anyone aged between 66 and 70.

Anyone else called for service must attend unless they can show good reason why they should be excused. Failure to do so can result in a fine of up to £1,000. However, it seems that some courts will overlook this, believing that forcing someone to sit on a jury is likely to cause more problems than it is worth.

Finance There is no pay for jury service. Travelling expenses are paid and money is available to compensate people for loss of earnings. But this is a relatively low figure – and unless their employer covers their wages, many on jury service will be out of pocket.

■ Six weeks' later

Tessa knew that people are given the opportunity to do jury service usually just once in their life. She decided, therefore, that it would be a shame to miss this chance.

Tessa arrived at the Crown Court, joining the 30 to 40 other people who had been called on that day. After a short introduction, they were shown a video, explaining what will happen in court.

A court official then chose 15 people at random, including Tessa, and led them to Court 4, where a trial was about to begin.

Swearing in Once inside the courtroom, another random selection was made. Twelve of the 15 people present were told to sit in the jury box.

Again, Tessa was chosen. Each member of the jury was sworn in – but, just before this happened, both the prosecution and defence could challenge the choice of a person as a juror, if they had good reason.

I'M NOT *#@•%#* SWEARIN' IN!

❓ questions

5. Sometimes people selected for jury service are blind, deaf or have reading difficulties. What are the arguments in favour of and against allowing each of these people to serve? What do you feel the law should say about this?

Criminal law

Cause of death

During her two-week jury service, Tessa heard three cases. The first involved assault and the second, dangerous driving. The third was a charge of burglary and manslaughter.

■ Accused

The defendant
Graham Eden, aged 26

Charges
Burglary, contrary to Section 9(1) of the *Theft Act 1968* and manslaughter — that is, killing resulting from an unlawful and dangerous act.

Plea
Guilty to burglary. Not guilty to manslaughter.

■ The facts

On January 16th, Frank Bingham, aged 72, was alone in his house on Victoria Road. Around 3.45 p.m. a brick was pushed through a small pane of glass in the front door and a man entered the house. Mr Bingham walked into the hallway and asked the intruder what he was doing.

The man said that he was looking for cash. Shouting at Mr Bingham, he walked straight into the front room and started to search a small cupboard and then some shelves, pulling out the contents onto the floor. Mr Bingham said that he had no money in the house, other than £15 that he had in his pocket. The man took the money and left.

A witness later identified Graham Eden as the person she had seen running away from the house shortly before 4 p.m. His fingerprints were found on the front door and on several pieces of furniture. He was arrested two days later.

Immediately after the burglary Mr Bingham telephoned the police. Three officers were at his house in less than ten minutes. Two council workmen also arrived within an hour, called to repair the damage to Mr Bingham's front door.

Shortly after the police left his house, and about an hour and a half after the break in, Mr Bingham was taken ill. He had suffered a heart attack and was pronounced dead on arrival at hospital.

Evidence

Prosecution The chief witness called by the prosecution was Dr Geddes, who had examined Mr Bingham's body after he had died. He stated that, in his experience, the shock brought on by a stressful incident could last for at least an hour and a half, particularly for someone like Mr Bingham who suffered from a heart complaint.

Dr Geddes said that he believed that the shock and anxiety of the burglary undoubtedly brought on Mr Bingham's heart attack.

Defence Graham Eden did not give evidence, but lawyers for the defence called two witnesses – Dr Foster and Eileen Lewis, a neighbour.

Eileen Lewis stated that there was a considerable amount of noise outside Mr Bingham's house in the period immediately after the burglary. She heard several police sirens and loud banging at the front of the house as the door was being repaired.

Dr Foster, a heart specialist, said that stress brought on by the burglary would have subsided after 20 minutes, and could not be a cause of death one and

Assessing the evidence

The jury

The job of the jury in a criminal trial is to listen to the evidence and to decide whether the defendant is guilty or not guilty.

Proof Criminal cases of law require a higher level of proof than civil cases. Members of the jury are told by the judge that they should reach a verdict of guilty only if they are really sure of the defendant's guilt.

Verdict A judge will ask the jury to reach a unanimous verdict. However, if they have been deliberating for more than two hours, the judge may call the jury back into court and tell them that a majority verdict eleven or ten will be acceptable.

Secrecy Jurors are not allowed by law to discuss the case with anyone else either during or after the trial.

a half hours later. If anything, it was likely to be the presence of the police or the workmen that triggered the attack.

Summing up

The judge told the jury that they must consider the opinions that they had heard in court very carefully. If they were certain that Mr Bingham died as a direct consequence of the burglary, they should find Graham Eden guilty of manslaughter. On the other hand, if they felt that Dr Foster was correct, or even that he may be correct, they should find the defendant not guilty.

? questions

1. On the information that you have been given, would you find Graham Eden guilty or not guilty of manslaughter?

2. It has been suggested that juries should give reasons for their verdict. What do you think would be the advantages and disadvantages of this idea?

Civil law

This unit looks at the way in which a case of civil law may be dealt with.

Taking a case to court

■ On the bench

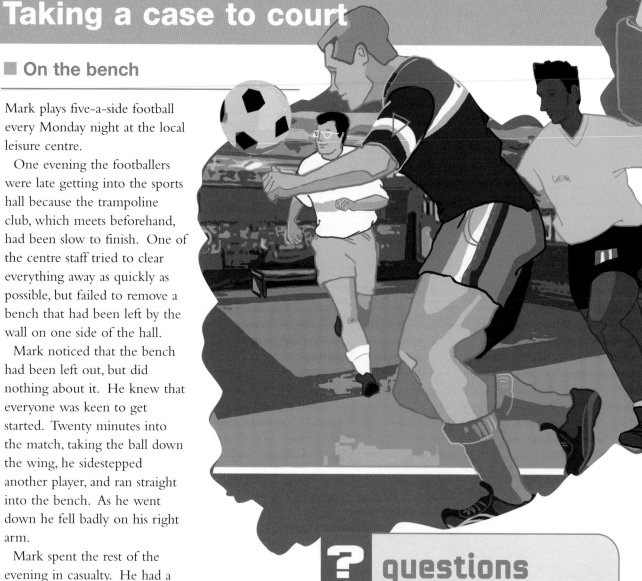

Mark plays five-a-side football every Monday night at the local leisure centre.

One evening the footballers were late getting into the sports hall because the trampoline club, which meets beforehand, had been slow to finish. One of the centre staff tried to clear everything away as quickly as possible, but failed to remove a bench that had been left by the wall on one side of the hall.

Mark noticed that the bench had been left out, but did nothing about it. He knew that everyone was keen to get started. Twenty minutes into the match, taking the ball down the wing, he sidestepped another player, and ran straight into the bench. As he went down he fell badly on his right arm.

Mark spent the rest of the evening in casualty. He had a small cut above his eye, his shin was heavily bruised, and his right arm was broken just above the wrist.

Counting the cost Mark is a self-employed builder and, because of his injuries, had to take a month off work – without pay. A week before the accident Mark had bought tickets for a music festival, costing £100 each, for himself and his girlfriend. With a broken arm, he was unable to drive and the tickets were not used.

? questions

1. The actions of the leisure centre staff, the trampoline club, his team-mates, the opposition and Mark himself all led in some way to the accident. Who do you think has the main responsibility? Explain why.

2. What do you think Mark should do next? You may find the information on the right-hand side of this page helpful.

Next

Mark phoned the Community Legal Service who gave him the names of local solicitors specialising in cases of personal injury. He rang one of these and made an appointment, deliberately selecting a firm where the first half-hour consultation was free.

Advice The solicitor said she believed that Mark had a good case for claiming **damages** against the local authority, which ran the leisure centre, as the staff there had a legal duty to make sure that the sports facilities were safe for people to use.

However, the solicitor explained, taking action of this kind could be time consuming and stressful, particularly if the case went to court.

Costs The solicitor said that, under what is known as the 'no win, no fee' scheme, Mark would not be charged a fee if his case did not succeed – although he would face some expense in getting a doctor's report and travelling to court, if the case went to trial.

However, if he lost the court case, he would almost certainly have to pay the other side's costs. These could be at least £1,000. Insurance was available to cover this, but the cost of taking this out would be quite expensive.

If he won, as the solicitor believed he would, he could receive several thousand pounds in damages – but these could be reduced, the solicitor pointed out, if the court decided that Mark had contributed

Taking a case to court

■ Here to help

Citizens Advice Bureau (CAB) There are offices in most towns and cities, providing free and confidential advice on all kinds of problems.

Solicitors These are trained lawyers able to give advice on legal problems, take action on their client's behalf and represent them in court.

Help in finding a local solicitor with experience of dealing with the problem in question is available from the Law Society and the Community Legal Service (CLS). The Law Society may be reached on 020 7242 1222 and www.solicitors-online.com. The CLS website is www.justask.org.uk, telephone 0845 608 1122.

Law centres Staffed by qualified lawyers, they give advice and may be able to take on a case in much the same way as a solicitor, sometimes at a much lower charge. However, there are only just over 50 law centres in the whole of England and Wales and most are located in inner-city areas.

Legal costs Arrangements to help people with the cost of civil legal cases have changed in recent years. In 2000 a new legal services scheme took the place of what used to be called legal aid. Public funding is no longer available for help with certain types of legal problem, which includes cases of personal injury. These are now handled on a 'no win, no fee' basis (see below).

to the accident himself. Under the 'no win, no fee' arrangement, his solicitor's costs would be deducted from his award of damages.

 **question**

3. What options does Mark face? Which one would you recommend that he took? Explain why.

 keywords

Damages
Money awarded by a court to compensate someone for the loss or injury they have suffered.

Civil law

The County Court

■ Seeking a settlement

Mark puts together evidence to support his claim. This includes his account of what happened, statements from two other players in the five-a-side team, a doctor's report, and details of his losses arising from the accident. These are sent to the solicitor acting for the local authority, which runs the leisure centre.

```
Special damages
Loss of earnings; 4 weeks @ £450
a week £1,800.00
Replacing glasses, damaged in
the accident £100.00
Taxi fares, when unable to
drive £40.00
Music festival tickets,
unused £200.00

General damages
Pain and suffering from broken
arm, a badly bruised shin, minor
bruising to the head.
```

Shortly afterwards, Mark's solicitor receives copies of the evidence obtained by the local authority, indicating why they feel they should not be held responsible for Mark's accident.

■ Evidence in court

As both sides have been unable to settle their disagreement, the case now moves to court – about six months after the accident took place.

Mark's solicitor is claiming that Mark's injuries were caused by the negligence of the leisure centre staff.

Proof If Mark is to be successful his solicitor must show:
- that staff at the leisure centre had responsibility to make sure that the sports hall was safe for playing football
- that they failed in this responsibility by not putting the bench away, and
- that this was the cause of Mark's injuries.

County courts

County courts deal with a wide range of civil disputes. Most cases are brought by people trying to recover debts or money owed as part of a contract. However, county courts also handle cases involving personal injury, family matters, divorce and discrimination not connected with work.

Although the judge usually wears a wig and robes, other people in court are dressed in ordinary clothes.

Small claims track For personal injury claims up to £1,000 and for most other claims up to £5,000, there is a simpler procedure designed to save time and allow people to conduct their case without a solicitor. A typical case of this kind could be a holiday that did not live up to expectations.

The case is heard in an ordinary room, rather like an office. The hearing is quite informal – the judge does not wear a wig or a gown – and both sides are seated around a table. The judge will try to draw out the relevant information and having reached a verdict will explain the reasons for his or her decision.

? question

1. Put yourself in the position first of Mark's solicitor, and then the lawyer acting for the local authority. List the arguments that you think each side could make in support of their case.

■ Verdict

The judge must decide, on the basis of the evidence, what happened in the sports hall that night – and who had responsibility in law for the injuries that Mark received.

In a civil matter such as this, the case must be proved 'on the balance of probabilities'. This is a lower level of proof than is required in a criminal court, where the jury must be sure that the defendant is guilty.

Guidelines for damages All judges use the same guide when awarding damages for injury. The current guide, in 2002, states that damages for a broken arm should be between £3,500 and £9,500.

However, if the judge decides that Mark should receive damages but that he contributed to the accident in some way himself, then the damages may be reduced. This is known as contributory negligence.

? questions

2. Now put yourself in the position of the judge. What verdict would you give in this case? Give the reasons for your judgement.

3. If you decide that the leisure centre staff were negligent, what would you award Mark in damages? Again give your reasons.

keywords

General damages
The name given to damages that cannot be precisely calculated – for example, the effect of pain and suffering.

Negligence
Careless action, or lack of action, causing someone loss or injury.

Special damages
Damages arising from an incident that can be specifically calculated – for example loss of earnings as a result of an accident.

GCSE Citizenship Studies

This unit is written specifically for those students who are taking the OCR GCSE Short Course in Citizenship Studies. It outlines the nature of the course and provides guidance on the examination and coursework.

The OCR course

The OCR GCSE Short Course provides you with an opportunity to obtain an approved qualification in Citizenship Studies.

The course consists of one tier covering grades A★ to G. Candidates who gain grades G to D will have achieved an award at Foundation Level. Candidates gaining grades C to A★ will have achieved an award at Intermediate Level.

Your Citizenship Studies course will probably be taught as a regular and separate timetabled subject. However, you are also encouraged to use information you have gained from other subjects as well. It is also worth remembering that any work you do either in school or the community may also be useful here – particularly as the basis for your coursework.

■ Coursework and the examination

Assessment for the course is divided into two parts – coursework and written examination.

Coursework Candidates are required to submit two pieces of coursework, which together make up 40 per cent of the total mark.

The written examination This consists of one paper lasting 1hr 30 minutes. It has three sections and accounts for 60 per cent of the marks.
- *Section A:* multiple choice and short answer questions carrying 20 per cent of the total mark.
- *Section B:* questions based on issues covered in the source book that will be sent to schools by the examining board six weeks before the examination. Candidates can take the source book into the exam, but no additional materials are permitted. This section again carries 20 per cent of the total mark.
- *Section C:* questions based on a candidate's reflections and understanding of action they have undertaken within the school and/or the wider community. This again counts for 20 per cent of the mark.

Assessment objectives The three assessment objectives are set out in the course syllabus, as follows.

You will be required to:
- demonstrate your knowledge and understanding of events of current interest; roles, rights and responsibilities; communities and identities; democracy and government; and relate them appropriately to individual, national and global contexts
- obtain, explain, and interpret different kinds of information, including that from the media, in order to discuss, form and express an opinion formally and in writing and demonstrate your ability to analyse and present evidence on a variety of issues, problems and events
- plan and evaluate the citizenship activities in which you have participated, and demonstrate an understanding of your own contribution to them, as well as recognising the views, experiences and contributions of others.

Coursework

Candidates are required to submit two pieces of coursework for examination. Each one must not be more than 800 words in length and carries 20 per cent of the total mark.

The pieces are each referred to separately as *Coursework A* and *Coursework B*. They are quite different, and are explained in detail below.

■ Coursework A

Coursework A is an account of your involvement in a school- or community-based activity.

School-based activities include community or

environmental projects, taking part in a play or other large project, being a member of the school council or a reading partner.

Community activities cover charity work, support for a local group, the Duke of Edinburgh Award or membership of a youth group or council.

In your account you must explain: what you did, why you did it, what you learnt from the activity, and what it did for others.

You must also outline the background and context of your activity and try to make sure that the examiner can see what you have learnt or gained. It is a good idea to highlight the problem that you faced and how you tried to overcome it. The examiner will also be interested to know how you might build on your experience.

You might also like to keep a diary or logbook of what you did and take some photographs to illustrate what the activity involved.

■ Coursework B

In *Coursework B* the exam board asks candidates to write an account comparing two sources of information on a citizenship issue of their choice.

Every section in this book is based on a citizenship issue of some kind, such as crime, race, poverty and the environment. A citizenship issue is a question that affects society as a whole, on which there is some disagreement over how to proceed. For example, *how should we care for the elderly?* or *who is responsible for reducing pollution?*

In your assignment you must:
• summarise the views expressed in each of the sources that you have chosen
• set the main issues in context, by explaining the background to the events in question and relating to the local, national, or global picture
• identify and explain any bias that is evident in your sources
• express and justify your views on the matter in question, and suggest how you think the situation might develop.

■ Supervision

You should receive guidance from your teacher – particularly when selecting the topic for your coursework and drawing up an overall plan. However, your reflections, judgements and conclusions must be all your own.

■ Presentation

Any work that you use must be acknowledged. You should do this by writing a bibliography at the end of your assignment indicating the author and the name of the publisher. Anything directly quoted should be shown using speech marks.

All work submitted for moderation must be in an A4 flat card file or document wallet, not a ring binder. Mark your work with the:
• centre number
• centre name
• candidate number
• subject title and code
• assignment title, i.e. *Coursework A* or *B*.

Volunteering

There is huge scope for getting involved in, or volunteering for, community activities. If you are not clear about what you would like to do, help is available from a number of websites, including Community Service Volunteers *(www.csv.org.uk)* and the National Centre for Volunteering *(www.volunteering.org.uk)*. These give ideas and guidance on volunteering opportunities in your own area. There is also a Volunteer Bureaux in most towns and cities. Details are available from the phone book and your local library.

There are certain practical questions that you will also need to consider. How much time can you afford? Are you able to make a regular commitment, or would it be better to volunteer for just one event? How far are you prepared or able to travel? Will you make the arrangements alone, or would you prefer to volunteer with a friend?

You will also need to plan how you will use your volunteering experience in your coursework. This is likely to involve background research and a discussion with the organisers or the people with whom you volunteer. You may also need to go back to assess the impact or effect of what you have done.

GCSE Citizenship Studies
The examination

The paper is divided into three sections and candidates are expected to answer all questions. All three assessment objectives (see pages 140–141) are tested in the paper. *Sections A and B test assessment objectives I and II. Section C tests objective III.*

■ Section A

The questions in this section are made up of:
- five multiple-choice questions, each worth one mark
- ten short or one-word answer questions, each worth one mark
- four short response answers, two worth two marks, and two worth one mark.

Multiple-choice Put a ring around the number of the definition (1,2,3,4) that matches the term.

A1 *What is meant by the term globalisation?* **(1)**

1. A global agreement to encourage sustainable development.
2. A move towards a single currency for members of the European Community.
3. A declaration of the United Nations to encourage greater international security.
4. The trend for large businesses and the media to operate across the world.

Short or one-word answers

A2 *State what is meant by the term pressure group.* **(1)**

A3 *State one way in which a political party differs from a pressure group.* **(1)**

Short response answers

Sam buys a plastic model kit for her son, Danny. She gives it to him when he gets home, and he starts to put it together straightaway. Danny soon realises that a piece is missing. Sam checks to make sure it has not fallen on the floor and decides that the kit must have been incomplete when she bought it.
Sam asks your advice on what to do next.

A4 *Circle the statement 1, 2, or 3 that gives the best advice and give one reason to explain why you have chosen it.*

1 Send the kit to the manufacturer and ask for it to be exchanged for one that is complete.

2 Report the matter to the police.

3 Take the kit back to the shop and ask for her money back.

Reason
....
....
....
....
....
....   **(2)**

■ Section B

Section B has four questions – two each worth six marks, and two each worth four marks.
Some weeks before the exam you will receive a source book. Your teacher will help you understand the information in this booklet and you will be allowed to annotate it with your own notes. You need to have the source book with you in the exam.
Questions in section B require you to show that you are able to understand and interpret the information in the source book.

B1 Study document 4 and answer the question that follows.

Document 4

Halim's story

Halim is a journalist from Algeria. Two years ago he wrote a series of articles criticising those religious groups who were trying to stop Algeria from becoming too westernised. He said the people should be allowed to adopt western values if they chose to, and that religious hardliners were wrong to try to prevent women from having more rights.

From then on, it seemed, Halim was a marked man. There were two attempts on his life, his newspaper's office was bombed and threats were made to his wife and child.

He asked for protection from the government. Help was promised, but his life became no safer. Government officials themselves were often targets for attack.

Under the pretence of going on a family holiday to Egypt, Halim took his wife and daughter to Cairo and then on to London, where he claimed political asylum.

Using **source 1** from your source book, explain whether Halim would be likely to qualify for refugee status in the United Kingdom. Give one reason for your decision. **(4)**

Source 1

The Convention Relating to the Status of Refugees, passed by the United Nations in 1951, defines a refugee as follows:

A refugee is a person who is outside their country and cannot return because of a well-founded fear of persecution for reasons of race, nationality, membership of a particular social group or political opinion.

Someone who does not fully meet this test may still be allowed to stay by being given Exceptional Leave to Remain. This is a special agreement that allows a person to stay in Britain if sending them home would seem to be very cruel or unkind.

■ Section C

Section C has three questions worth two, three and 15 marks.

The 15-mark question requires an essay-style answer and carries an extra four marks for communication skills, making it worth 19 marks in total.

C1 *Using examples taken from your studies and from any school or community action that you have taken part in, state **three** things that you could do in a democracy to influence decision-makers.* **(3)**

C2 *'All young people, at some stage in their school life, should be required to undertake voluntary work of some kind.'*

Write an essay to show how far you agree with this statement. **(15)**

In your answer you may use examples from your studies and from any school or community action project that you have taken part in.

Index